Mona,
A Mother's Story

GINETTE BUREAU, PH.D.

BALBOA.
PRESS

A DIVISION OF HAY HOUSE

Balboa Press books may be ordered through booksellers or by contacting:

Balboa Press
A Division of Hay House
1663 Liberty Drive
Bloomington, IN 47403
www.balboapress.com
1 (877) 407-4847

Because of the dynamic nature of the Internet, any web addresses or links contained in this book may have changed since publication and may no longer be valid. The views expressed in this work are solely those of the author and do not necessarily reflect the views of the publisher, and the publisher hereby disclaims any responsibility for them.

The author of this book does not dispense medical advice or prescribe the use of any technique as a form of treatment for physical, emotional, or medical problems without the advice of a physician, either directly or indirectly. The intent of the author is only to offer information of a general nature to help you in your quest for emotional and spiritual well-being. In the event you use any of the information in this book for yourself, which is your constitutional right, the author and the publisher assume no responsibility for your actions.

Any people depicted in stock imagery provided by Thinkstock are models, and such images are being used for illustrative purposes only.
Certain stock imagery © Thinkstock.

Print information available on the last page.

ISBN: 978-1-5043-5663-3 (sc)
ISBN: 978-1-5043-5664-0 (e)

Balboa Press rev. date: 05/09/2016

Publisher's note:

In 1970, the year this story opens, Ginette Bureau and her American-born husband, André, were living in a small town in the province of Quebec with their two children — Francis, aged six, and Mona, aged four. Their story, and all the events in this book, are true. However, to protect the privacy of the people involved as much as possible, all first names have been changed and all family names dropped.

Mona, A Mother's Story

It's a story about a miracle. In the seventies, I was told by doctors that my 4 year old daughter had a few months to live. I searched for a way to fully make the most of whatever time we had left. My prayers were answered. I started treating her like she was going to grow up. She was much happier. I blocked my ears to the medical prognosis and followed my inner voice. Mona grew up. I wrote her story which I gave to her for her 12th birthday.

Today, science is demonstrating the power of the mind over the body. In a scientific program presented in *Les grands documentaires,* researchers gave evidence that the placebo's effect is powerful. Injecting words instead of medication actually works. They show how words can change the function of our brain.

The link between our body and spirit is being illustrated by the progress in neurosciences. Many experiences prove that the brain according to its belief is able to secrete certain drugs to eliminate pain for example. There is no doubt, what we think and what we feel influences our cure. The psychological and the affective context have an important effect on the treatment. The biological factors are important, but words, body language, attitude, human relationships and beliefs are showing that the spirit and body are related in a mysterious way.

When Mona's life was in danger, a very powerful intuition came to me as a grace of God - supernatural force and I put all these suggestions in practice to save her. In those days, I had to keep my inner attitude a secret from the doctors so they would not treat me as an overly anxious mother.

Years later, on her paediatrician's demand, I published Mona's story. He suggested the book to his student's doctors so they would change their bedside manners forever.

I hope that reading about this miracle will help you believe in a mysterious power. It has nothing to do with the ego, it comes from deep down, an infinite Source. I hope you have access to it as I did when living and writing Mona's story.

Ginette Bureau, February 2016.

Part I

"Mommy, mommy . . ."

My four-year-old daughter was calling me. I had trouble waking up. Why do children always wake up early when their parents have gone to bed late? It was just three in the morning.

"Come here, Mona! Come and see Mom."

She was hot with fever and crying. She said that she ached all over. Her arm hurt.

"Did you fall down?"

"I don't know . . ."

Since she's always on the go, there was no way of telling where or when she had hurt herself.

"Did you play ball with the big kids again?"

She nodded. "But I didn't play today, it happened the other day. I got hit with the ball and my arm hurt a lot . . ."

"Why didn't you tell Mommy when you hurt yourself?"

André woke up. "You're asking her too many questions. Can't you see that she's sick?"

"I know she's sick, poor baby. And I'm starting to worry. First those glands in her neck and now this fever."

"You called the pediatrician about her glands, didn't you? What did he say?"

"He told me to give her aspirin and use hot compresses for the pain. And he told me to take her to the hospital if we were worried about her."

Hospitals in Quebec had been on strike, and on the radio they were asking people to go only in cases of emergency. I didn't like the idea of sitting around in a crowded waiting room and having to see just any doctor; all the same I decided to go the next day, and for the time being I gave Mona an aspirin. In her father's arms she was already starting to calm down.

I was afraid and worried about Mona, but André had already fallen asleep. Anyway, I knew he would just say that I worried too much. But I wanted to tell him that we'd been neglecting the children ever since we'd started house-hunting, and that Mona didn't always eat properly, even though he knew that as well as I did. Lately we'd been trying to break her of the bad habit of snacking between meals and eating only when she liked what was on the menu. Maybe it was just my imagination, but in the past few days she'd liked what I'd been serving less and less. Tomorrow I'd make one of her favourite dishes. I stroked her head one last time; she was less feverish. I slipped under the covers and made sure, since she was lying between us, to cover her lightly so she wouldn't be too hot.

The next morning, the day after Thanksgiving, we were waiting our turn in the emergency room which was being reserved for children during the strike. Boys and girls were whimpering and crying. Mona was quieter than usual; she looked unhappy and didn't say much. But already I was less worried. Soon they would tell me what the problem was and what I should do about it.

We got an elderly doctor. Faced with so many children, he seemed exhausted. He hardly asked any questions and started his examination right away. I watched his face — that's my way of figuring out how serious things are. He hadn't stopped frowning since we had walked into his office, and he gave me a sidelong glance when he saw all the bruises on Mona's legs, especially a big one on her bottom. Even I was surprised when I saw it. I hadn't noticed it, since Mona always insists on getting dressed by herself. She must have hurt herself the night before, although the baby-sitter hadn't mentioned it. I asked Mona what had happened to her. The doctor looked as though he suspected me of child abuse.

"Sometimes I get bruises without realizing it," I stammered.

He felt her stomach and examined her from head to toe. Every time he looked at me, I was sure he was going to accuse me of criminal negligence. If only I'd stayed home last night!

"What's the matter? What's wrong with her?"

"Your daughter will have to stay in the hospital."

"But what about the strike?" I opened my mouth to say something more, but the doctor had disappeared. I had thought this would just be a routine visit; they would tell me what was wrong, prescribe some pills, and then she would go home,

4

practically cured. This time nobody was saying a word, and I got the feeling that it was better not to ask any questions. Still, I had to do something.

"Come on, Mona, we'll go call Daddy."

But they had already returned for her. Things were happening much too fast. I didn't understand any of it.

"They'll take good care of you, my kitten," I tried to explain. "Mommy will be close by. I'll come back and see you with Dad after dinner." But when I held her in my arms, I couldn't hold back my tears.

"Why are you crying, Mom?" she asked.

I told myself to be more reasonable. Mona left me like a big girl, head held high, as if off on an adventure. She wanted to look around and take everything in, while I stood there watching her disappear. I felt like I was being robbed.

People were coming and going in the emergency room, taking no notice of me. The nurses and doctors put on smiles that looked mechanical. They were used to this kind of thing! Suddenly there wasn't enough air to breathe in the lobby.

Outside it was cloudy, and the fresh air made me feel a little less numb. I began walking, not really knowing where I was going. If only André was with me . . . I was annoyed at being alone, but I was too upset to get mad. I knew he would show up. I dried my tears so people wouldn't see them, but at the same time I wanted to tell everyone how stupid it all was. Mothers complain that their kids are too much work, but as soon as someone takes one away, we start to cry. We can't stand the endless racket they make, but as soon as the house is quiet we don't know what to do with ourselves. We want them to be grown-ups and babies at the same time.

André usually thinks I worry needlessly when the children are sick, but this time he took things very seriously. He left his classes to come and be with us. Now all three of us sat together, waiting for the verdict. A doctor came in calling our names.

"I'd like to see you alone for a minute. Leave your daughter in the playroom."

Never before had I felt the menace so close. I was afraid of how I was going to react.

"You have other children, I hope," he asked brusquely.

He was going too fast, yet his preamble seemed to last forever. Why didn't he get to the point? I'd already decided that I didn't like this doctor. Everything about him told me that he had terrible news for us.

"I see you have a son." And he paused. I couldn't stand listening to the sound of his breathing.

"Your daughter has leukemia. Do you know anything about it?"

Just the word itself made me think it was something serious, but I had never known anyone who had actually died of the disease. But André had once watched a five-year-old girl die of it, slowly, week by week. It was the sickness he had always secretly dreaded. He had guessed it was leukemia even before the doctor had spoken, and he nodded his head. I looked at him, I looked at the doctor, I tried to understand.

The doctor went on, "The tests aren't complete, but it's almost certain." Then I heard him say, "You should try to get used to the fact as quickly as possible. The average length of survival is only six months to two years, I'm afraid."

Enough! I wanted to scream. Not another word! I understood, I understood only too well.

The doctor began telling me about another mother who had brought her child to the hospital when the child had reached the final stage. The mother knew it and had resigned herself to the fact. Resigned! I hated that word. The story made me feel sick. I couldn't imagine bringing your child in just like that, with no more pain, or almost none, just because you'd been warned months earlier. What difference did that make?

When they talked about the specialist who would treat Mona, I did my best to listen. My daughter was to receive the best medical attention. We wanted her to go to Boston, to a special centre. But the doctor told us that it would be too hard on her because of the travel and the fatigue, and that she would receive the same treatment here. He talked about remission. Most children who suffered from leukemia had one, then another that was shorter, and others still shorter each time . . . until the medication no longer worked. I tried to keep my head clear. Was this really happening? I hid my head in my hands. If only my heart would stop beating so hard.

The doctor let us catch our breath. Finally he said, "We can at least be thankful that dying from this disease entails very little suffering."

I hated that doctor because he was talking to us about death.

"During remission, children seem to be in quite good health, enough to convince you that nothing is wrong. They can lead an almost normal life. But you must not mistake it for a cure, because you would only suffer more in the end."

All right, all right! We understood, the disease was incurable. But Mona was waiting for us on the other side of the office door. I wanted to stay and go at the same time. The doctor told us to take our time.

How short two years seemed all of a sudden. What was two years? Just a few months, a few days, a few moments. And meanwhile I was hesitating about opening that door and going out to see her. Shakily, I tried to stand up. I felt as if I had just been hit over the head, but I did manage to walk. As I opened the door, Mona came toward us, pale and worried. I wished I had a mask to cover my face so she wouldn't see my pained grin. Have you ever noticed that it's almost impossible to hide your thoughts from a child? Mona seemed to be trying to read our eyes and I tried not to think of death, otherwise she would sense it too. I held her very close. I wanted my arms to tell her, Mona, you can count on Mom. I'll help you, I love you so much.

My husband picked her up in his arms and we walked down the hall, simply because we had to do something. Before this I had only come to the hospital to have children. And then when I walked down the hall, I felt like a queen, as if I was the only woman in the world who could give birth. But this time it was different . . .

I glanced at the other sick children around us. A little girl had burns all over her body. Lucky her; it was only burns. The nurses at the nursing station watched us go by, and I wondered if they knew. Their composure drove me crazy and I wanted to scream something at them, but I couldn't say a word. I could scarcely keep my teeth from chattering and I didn't dare touch André for fear of feeling his body tremble too. I couldn't even look at him; we might both break down.

At the end of the hallway was a little counter. We leaned on it and sat Mona between us. André held her by the waist with fatherly tenderness. We each took her hand. We tried to grasp what was happening to us. It seemed that Mona had only been born yesterday and already . . . it was impossible! She looked at us, each in turn, as she played with our fingers. Suddenly, as if she understood everything, she joined our hands. And that touch united us with the sudden force of an electric shock.

Heartbroken, we tried to distract her. I thought of all those times when she had wanted to snack between meals, and I had forced her to wait until supper. How sick she must have felt! Her very blood had become a menace to her. I remembered the times when she had been tired and sulked, and when I would tell her harshly, "Mona, perk up. Be like the other kids, make up a game, play a little. Don't just mope around all day doing nothing."

Her brother had just started school and she missed him terribly. Sometimes in the afternoons she preferred to sleep rather than go out and play. Considering that she used to love to run and play outside, I should have realized that something was wrong. How could I have been so blind? What sort of mother was I?

They were going to bathe Mona in cold water because her fever was climbing. We took advantage of the break to go out for awhile and we promised her we would come back right after supper. She went off with the nurse, totally trusting, and we headed for the exit. I thought I'd never make it. Finally we reached the car and I couldn't hold back my tears any longer. André begged me to get hold of myself. But no words could cut through my despair.

There is no hell like the loss of hope, and I was staring hell in the face. Never before had I felt so low. I was twenty-seven years old and I felt as if life were absurd. I looked around at the beautiful houses and I hated them. What good were beautiful houses and new dresses? There were people who actually lived for those things! I was sorry for every moment I had spent on useless things. I was mad at myself; I was mad at the whole world.

André drove through the streets of the town. Then, as if guided by intuition, he took me to the home of one of my closest girlfriends. Together the two of us had danced, partied and celebrated life and love. Her daughter was four years old, the same age as Mona, and as we drove up to the house she was outside skipping rope. I had to struggle to get hold of myself. Other people's kids had the right to live, even if mine . . . I was becoming incoherent again, mumbling bits and pieces of sentences. Finally a few words came out.

"Why Mona? What did I do to deserve this? Imagine living with the knowledge that she'll die in a year or two. How can I live with her counting the days she has left?"

Ghislaine didn't know what to do so she made supper, just for the sake of doing something. She asked me to eat with them. She listened to my cries for help, struggled to find words, and finally asked, "Why are you always talking about the future?"

"I can't help it. When she's in good health, I'll have to keep telling myself, it's only for a little while, don't get your hopes up, she's done for, there's nothing you can do, *nothing!*"

"But who are you to say what will happen two years from now?"

When I heard those words, I stopped crying. Hoping that she would argue and convince me, I countered, "This isn't the first case of leukemia the doctors have come across. They know how it works."

Ghislaine wasn't to be discouraged. She kept looking for a way to help. "Why don't you try to live for today, just for today? You know, if we all started thinking about what was going to happen to us in the future . . . ." She paused for a moment and continued, "Today she's alive, even if she is in the hospital. Go and see her, play with her, reassure her. Tomorrow, you'll deal with whatever happens. Don't try to live something that hasn't happened yet."

Her words soothed me. The knots in my stomach were loosening and I was breathing more easily. When I thought about it, everything she said made sense, but without giving false hopes either. She was right. Who really knew what the future would bring, and where we would be in a couple of years? Why make

9

myself sick worrying so much? Where would I find the strength and the courage to take care of my daughter if I did that?

Determined to live one day at a time, I opened the door to the pediatrics ward. Mona had fallen asleep on a sofa — a wine-red sofa, almost violet. She was wearing a white nightie. Her black curly hair framed her face and made her look even paler. She slept . . . as if in a coffin. I couldn't help seeing a coffin. Already I was giving in. Here I had wanted to live each day, one day at a time. What had happened to my determination? Mona was breathing, she was there. I had to live every moment. Live only for the present.

André had become very nervous; he couldn't stand waiting any longer. In a hospital, it seems as though you're always waiting for something. This time it was the doctor, who had said he would be there to look after Mona's transfer to another hospital. André paced and talked a little with Mona. He kept saying that he hated hospitals and the way they smelled, and that he was concerned about our six-year-old son Francis who was waiting for us at a friend's house. Finally he kissed us both and walked off. I knew that Francis, a high-strung, nervous boy, would be anxious, and that I'd be better off letting André leave. But why didn't he tell me — even if he was a man — that it was breaking his heart too, and that once he knew that I was a little stronger, he could let himself go? He never did tell me where he went to cry that night.

My brother was working as a nurse at the same hospital, and he arrived just as I was struggling through a story that I was telling Mona, trying my best to keep my voice steady. I saw by the way he looked at Mona that he too had learned his lesson about leukemia. He must already have seen children die of it. I was irritated and I didn't really know why. He did his best to hide his feelings, but I guess I knew my brother too well. Even though he was always enthusiastic and liked to cheer up his patients, tonight he wasn't up to it. His experience in dealing with children helped him to play and joke with Mona. But all his experience hadn't taught him how to keep his sister from reading in his eyes the tragic end that awaited us.

He anticipated my questions.

"They wouldn't let me see her file at the desk. It's all too close. It wouldn't be right if I knew before you."

Suddenly I had the feeling that they weren't telling me everything. That he knew a lot more that I did. I didn't know which way to turn. My heart pounded and all my resolutions went up in smoke. If I listened to reason and science, I would despair; but if I listened to my own heart, I would hope. I was sorry that Mona had to see me this way. My face burning, I managed to ask weakly, "What about the remissions? At least I ought to be that lucky."

My brother was upsetting me and he knew it. I could see that as far as he was concerned, all leukemia patients ended up the same way. And because he loved and understood me so well, he was strong enough to avoid running into me during Mona's long illness.

At the desk, tensions were rising. I asked the nurse what was keeping the doctor. She answered me coldly, "You know, this isn't the first case of leukemia we've ever treated here."

It was getting late; something was wrong. The doctor must be running into trouble with the transfer. I heard the telephone calls followed by exasperated sighs. I shuttled back and forth between the desk and Mona. The entire hold-up was due to the fact that the doctor who had told us the bad news was from another hospital, and had been dealing with us only because of the strike. He had hurt us badly, but he seemed conscientious enough; after all, he hadn't hidden anything from us. That was why we had decided to entrust Mona to him. He would be the pediatrician in charge. But it looked as though someone, somewhere, wasn't in agreement. I was glad André wasn't there. He would have wanted to speed things up and force the issue. But I didn't want to rush anything. I began to wonder if we had made the right decision. Then I regained my composure. Everything would work out.

The doctor finally arrived. "Everything's ready. You can take your daughter to the other hospital."

His face was drawn and he looked tired and irritable. Out of pride — and because I didn't want to inconvenience him any more — I didn't tell him that André had left, that he had had enough of waiting, that I didn't have any way of getting around...

Just then, the door swung open and my uncle walked in.

"You're just in time. I need your help."

He was glad to help out; after all, that was why he had come. He wrapped Mona in a blanket and drove us to the other hospital.

In Admitting, I had to fill out a series of forms, get out my insurance cards — all with Mona on my knees, whimpering the whole time. I was in the middle of digging through my purse when I heard my mother's voice. I thought I must be dreaming.

"Over here, Mother."

I had called her during the day to tell her what the doctor suspected, but I never expected her to come. She hates driving at night, yet she drove seventy-five miles in the dark to be with me.

I handed Mona to her, just as I had done when I'd left the hospital after she was born. But this time there was no joy in our hearts. I had to swallow hard a few times before I could say hello to my sister-in-law who had come with her.

The intern appeared, carrying his bag.

"Please, not another examination."

"Hospital rules. Every patient must be examined at the time of admitting."

Mona gave me a dejected look.

"Doctor, my daughter has already been through enough tests today. She's been very good, but she's tired now. Could you keep it short?"

I won that battle. He did only what was absolutely necessary for his report, and at last I was able to calm Mona down.

"Come on, Mom's going to tuck you in."

I tried to set my tiredness aside as I told her all about the new hospital, explained why we had taken her there, and showed her all the other children sleeping without their mothers. I told her I loved her and that I'd be back tomorrow morning.

"Good night." I whispered. "Sweet dreams."

Then I had to answer a few questions about her eating habits and, thankfully, that was it.

In the lobby my mother was patiently waiting to take me home. As I dropped into a chair I felt empty, exhausted. I didn't even have the strength to speak. I tried to remember if I had had anything to eat that day. I looked around for my coat. Then my sister-in-law said, "I came to help you find a place."

God! I had forgotten all about moving. In two weeks the owner would reclaim the house we had been renting. Everything was coming at me at once.

My mother asked me if I wanted to go home. I hated the house when the children weren't there, but what good would it do to say so?

I went back and looked at Mona through the window of the door to her room. She was sleeping peacefully. It wouldn't be a bad idea to get a little rest myself. On the way home my mother and my sister-in-law talked, and every once in a while I felt obliged to answer their questions, more out of politeness than anything else. But in fact, I wanted to stop everything, right then. I'd had enough.

The car rocked me like a cradle. I tried to think of the sound of the engine, of the night, the stars, anything, as long as it was something else. I wanted to lose consciousness, to stop feeling with my body and my heart. It hurt too much . . .

"How are you doing, Ginette?"

"Fine, fine."

"We'll be there in a minute."

I shivered. I was afraid, afraid of not being strong enough.

When I saw our house, it felt as though I'd left it years ago. Inside, a couple of friends had come to keep André company, and the three of them had fixed a little snack. I saw that the door to the children's room was closed. I didn't want to go in to kiss Francis good night and face the other empty bed. Someone offered me a cup of coffee and I had a bite to eat. I was recovering a bit, enough to answer their questions. They loved Mona too, and they wanted to know what was happening.

With my cigarette and cup of coffee I became more sociable. I told them what had happened, and what was in store for the following day. The doctors would do a bone marrow biopsy, and only after that would they be able to establish a final diagnosis and decide on treatment.

"Maybe they made a mistake," our friends said.

That's exactly what I hoped with all my heart. But the doctors wouldn't have given us a piece of news like that without being sure. I pictured the doctors coming to tell me they had been mistaken; after all, doctors weren't infallible. If so, I figured I would kill the doctor who had given me the news that afternoon. No, that wouldn't be right. I'd be so happy that I'd throw a party and invite him.

I let myself daydream as my friends talked about finding us an apartment. But I wanted a house, not an apartment. I was tired of dragging our things from one place to the next. We were always moving because we didn't have enough money to pay the raise in rent, or because the owner wanted to take back his house. Whether we liked it or not, we always had to pack our suitcases and move on. I'd had enough. I wanted to settle down in my own house. We had found one that was perfect last week, but the down payment was too high. I had been mad at my father-in-law because he hadn't wanted to help us out. But it was probably better that way. It would have meant working part-time for the extra money, and from now on, I would spend all my time on Mona and the rest of the family. It was just one more disappointment — and a small one compared to everything else that had happened.

For the past four years we've lived in a small town where people have their own way of letting you know how they feel. If they like you, they'll do anything to help you. But there's a catch. People watch you going about your business, they keep an eye on you, they try to find out what you think and why you're doing what you do. Whether you like it or not, word travels fast. People here make a big production over their neighbours' lives. At parties, they gossip about each other in the most intimate detail and envy whoever knows the most. I'd never participated in my neighbours' practices before, but tonight I discovered how they can work for you — and against you.

Around the table, our friends were discussing an apartment they thought would be perfect for us. Incredibly enough, they had already started looking into it. They described the place and even made me want to live there. They were so persuasive that I promised to go see it first thing in the morning. They knew the landlady and would put in a good word for us. When they left, they told us that we could count on their help.

"Thanks for looking after Francis," we said.

As I closed the door, I felt terribly weary at the prospect of everything that had to be done the next day. I wanted to be alone and rest. I made the beds for my mother and my sister-in-law while they cleared the table. I was at the end of my rope and I felt hot and cold at the same time. I was anxious to get to sleep and stop thinking. When I turned off the last light, I stretched out on my bed in relief and my muscles finally began to relax.

I had just closed my eyes when the telephone rang. I didn't want to answer it; I wouldn't move another muscle today! But what if the call was from the hospital? I leaped from my bed and picked up the phone before the third ring.

"Hello! Sorry for calling this late. I heard what happened. Is it really true?"

Did everybody know already? The doctor had advised us not to tell outsiders what disease Mona had, but it looked as though his recommendation didn't matter much any more. The woman on the end of the line said that she knew something bad must have happened when my husband left work so suddenly. People claimed he had gone to the hospital because his daughter was sick.

"Is it really true? I was worried," she said.

In the name of friendship she wanted to know more. And at eleven o'clock at night because, of course, I might not be home tomorrow. In her concerned voice, she asked me to go through the torture of describing the worst moments of the day. Some concern! It was nothing but the need some people had to be the first on the block to know, the first to be on the scene of an accident. I was so angry that I wanted to hang up. But I told myself that we don't live alone on this planet, and that she might have truly wanted to share my misery. Since I wasn't smart enough to think of a lie in a hurry, since I was too upset to think clearly and afraid that my anger was caused by grief, not by this telephone call, I gave in. I described my day one more time. I gave in to her desire to know.

But my palms were sweaty and my whole body trembled. I sat down, got up again, my heart beating its own strange rhythm. She asked me questions, always wanting more details. The precise descriptions of my pain made me feel as if I was stoking it like a fire. And to top it all off, I had to listen to her shower me with pity.

"Poor Ginette! That was the last thing you needed. My goodness, what a tragedy it must be for you!"

When people feel sorry for me, I have a tendency to pity myself, too. Self-pity takes away my strength and destroys me. I had to get hold of myself, or it would swallow me whole. I gathered myself together and decided to put an end to the painful conversation.

Trying to sound assertive, but shaking the whole time, I told her, "Listen, we don't want it to get out. We don't want people to pity her (perhaps now she would understand), and most of all, we don't want our son to find out."

But I knew she'd talk anyway as soon as my back was turned.

If I'd been a child, I would have cried, jumped up and down and thrown a tantrum. I was furious, though I didn't really know why. Who could I get mad at? God? The doctor? This friend of mine? Or my husband, who didn't know how to react to my anger? Besides, I simply hurt too much. I threw myself on the bed and finally fell asleep with her words echoing in my ears: Poor Ginette! Don't forget, don't get your hopes up. You'll only suffer more. What a tragedy!

When I opened my eyes I felt as if a knife had been plunged into my heart as the memories of the previous day returned. What if it had been just a nightmare? Those things only happened in films or to the neighbours, not in our house, not to me. But reality hit hard. Thinking of all the things I had to do, I got up and went into the bathroom with one thought in mind: not to look too miserable. Whatever the cost, I had to pull myself together and put on a happy face.

Looking at myself in the mirror was a frightening experience. My eyes were red and puffy and my complexion ashen. It looked as though I'd been put through the wringer and not been given time to disguise the damage. All the same, I tried: ice cubes under my eyes to shrink the bags, a little make-up to put some life and colour in my face. Just as I was trying for the third time to draw that little black line under my eyes that my tears kept muddying every time, I heard sounds from my son's room. He couldn't see me like this. He'd want to know why I was crying. I started my make-up all over again, and this time I was determined to get it over with. And when Francis came in to kiss me, I promised myself that I'd never let him know how desperate the situation really was.

Off to visit the only vacant apartment in town that was both available and adequate, I wiped all other thoughts from my mind and prepared to meet the landlady who would be renting to us. She had raised her family by herself. Her husband was a bum and she had ended up throwing him out. Through hard work and saving, she had managed to buy two apartment buildings. She was ruthless when it came to money, especially her own. But if she liked you, I'd been told, there would be no problem. I knocked at her door, a little nervous, knowing how important it was to play my cards right if I wanted to have a roof over my daughter's head when she left the hospital.

I decided to use the story of my sick daughter to persuade her. As I spoke, I realized what a dreadful predicament I was in, and how much work lay before me. I'd have to divide myself into four people to be at the hospital, pack our things and set up the apartment all at the same time. I wanted so much to convince the landlady that I ended up crying and everyone with me wiped the tears from their eyes too.

I was mad at myself for getting carried away. I'd gone too far. But the landlady agreed to do some repairs and she tried to console me by telling me about a sick little boy she had known. I only listened with half an ear, but I remember that the boy had been cured because of the devoted care he had received from a particular nurse who believed in his recovery. Then the landlady gave me a piece of advice. "Keep an eye on the way she's treated. That's the most important thing."

And I left, relieved and satisfied by the agreement we had reached.

"I'm going to buy a little something for Mona," my mother said.

"That would be nice. I'll go back and pack everything she'll need at the hospital."

I stood alone in the children's room. It was lifeless, despite all of Mona and her brother's things. The slippers near the closet, the pyjamas thrown on the bed yesterday morning next to her favourite doll, the puzzle in one corner of the room. How many times had I told her to put away her puzzle? Why bother telling a child those things? What good did it do? If the child leaves, what then? Tenderly, I picked up the little puzzle. I felt like overturning everything in the room, but I controlled myself and tidied things up instead. I came across the bag where Mona kept her music book. Twice a week I took her to a piano teacher for fifteen minutes. What mother doesn't have lofty dreams for her children? I leafed through the music book, and my tears stained the pages. Cold sweat clung to my back. It was only ten o'clock in the morning and I'd already cried three times. I had the rest of the day to live through and I wondered where I would find the strength. Urged on by the thought that Mona was waiting for me, I put a few clothes in the suitcase and left.

André, my mother and I nervously walked down the hall to Mona's room. The doctor spotted us and came over, greeting us with a big smile. He looked great, full of vitality. You could tell it wasn't his child! Mona was in the treatment room, and as he took us there he explained the tests they had done that morning.

"Some bone marrow was siphoned from the hipbone. Don't worry, it hardly hurts at all. We used a light anesthetic. You can see her as soon as the lab tells us that the biopsy is good enough to do an analysis."

He went into the room. Before we had time to assimilate the information, he was back again.

"Go on in. Mona's awake and wants to see you."

Mona was lying on a little white table in a room that smelled of disinfectant and was full of sterilized instruments. She was smiling. Very proudly, she showed us the quarter the doctor had given her. She let us see the spot where they had done the biopsy. I kissed her and they motioned us to take her away.

We all went to the visitors' room. Mona was having trouble walking. She laughed and said that her legs felt all rubbery. We smiled and crowded around her to watch her open my mother's gift. She wanted to start colouring right away but her right arm was in a sling, and we all did our best to help her. She managed to hold her crayon in her left hand and laughed at the results. She seemed so eager to have a good time that I thought it might not be so serious after all.

As the doctor walked by, he said almost lightly, "I'll see you later when we have the results from the biopsy." Then he bent over and whispered to Mona. He had won her confidence, and I was glad that she liked him.

But his words echoed in the air. Quiet now, we all hung our hopes on that word "results."

André and I spent the day going from one window to the next, down one hallway and up another, sometimes carrying Mona in our arms. We made ourselves as inconspicuous as possible to keep from disturbing the ward, but we left Mona only for meals and her afternoon nap. Although we were still desperately trying to grasp what was happening to us, one thing was certain: never before had we been more intensely aware of the love that bound us to our daughter.

To ease our own misery, we contemplated the misery of others. It seemed as if we were already old hands in pediatrics and we knew about many of the cases. All the other parents talked with each other about their children, why they were there, and every day we inquired about each other's progress.

We met an older couple who had a nine-year-old daughter, their only child. She had fallen from her bicycle and gone into a coma. We all saw how often harmless-looking accidents could have far more serious consequences. She wouldn't die, but would she emerge from her coma? And if she did wake up, would she be normal again? Her parents spent the day with us, and that very evening, together we celebrated their daughter's first cries. According to the doctors, she was completely out of danger.

When someone asked us about our daughter's disease, we would say that we didn't really know, we were still waiting for the results. And people were disappointed by our uncertainty that prevented them from knowing how serious Mona's condition was.

Deep down, we knew the doctor was going to give us bad news. We had been waiting too long. I decided that this enforced waiting period was a trick of the trade, to make us assimilate the facts slowly. I went to inquire at the nursing station. It was already four o'clock and André was pacing like a caged beast. We

20

were watching the sun go down, thinking of all sorts of possibil ities, when the doctor finally came in and introduced us to a colleague, some sort of general practitioner who would be responsible for the well-being of the family as a whole.

I wished he would stop explaining how the family clinic worked and give me the results of the tests. I studied the doctor's face, trying to read behind his eyes. I'd be O.K. this time; I had already been through it all yesterday. I'd be strong, I kept telling myself. But if the news were good, he would have told us right away. I silenced the tiny voice that begged for it to be something less serious.

Then he got to the point. "The last tests have confirmed that your daughter has leukemia."

Silently I cursed the dirty trick. Yesterday he had told us that nothing was certain, just to leave us a little hope, and now he was snatching all hope away. My face stung as if someone had suddenly pulled a bandage off a fresh wound. But this time I intended to get a hold of myself more quickly, not like yesterday. I had to talk to him. It couldn't be as fatal as he said it was. He spoke of the treatment she would be undergoing, and I tried to make him admit that there was still some chance she would pull through.

"I don't really believe so," he said. "All the cases I'm acquainted with . . . well, they were terminal."

My mother saw the pain he was causing us. She burst out, "But there's no way you can tell how long she'll live."

The doctor answered, "Let me warn you against people who will try to convince you that she's cured when she's only in remission."

"Isn't there any hope?"

With a pencil, he drew a wide circle. Then he made a dot within the circle to stand for our tiny hopes. Of course, we weren't supposed to even count on that.

"It would be better to get used to the idea. That way, you'll suffer less every time she has a relapse."

"But how can anyone live knowing for certain that they're going to die? How can you talk about remissions and a normal life?"

"It takes a long time to get used to it."

21

It all rang hollow. Even if he did know what he was talking about, I still had the feeling that he didn't really mind making us suffer. They were all the same, these doctors. They liked to lay on the pain so they could comfort you better afterwards. But at the time I was afraid that he wasn't telling me everything, just to soften the blow. Maybe he was really telling us that she would die very soon, and I was just refusing to hear him. In my confusion I went from one extreme to the other, trying to interpret his gestures, the intonation of his voice or the look in his eyes.

I managed to calm down enough to listen to his biology lesson when my husband asked for information about the disease. The doctor seemed surprised, but then, obliging, he took a piece of paper and compared the profile of normal blood with Mona's blood. Obviously he wanted to be sure we understood just how serious her condition was.

"You see, the blood platelets must be maintained at an average level of two hundred thousand, and Mona's level is only two thousand. That's why her arm hurt so much when she was hit and the blood seeped in between the muscle and the bone. The platelets are what coagulates the blood."

I could picture her blood that would not coagulate, that kept flowing and flowing . . . I knew that I was becoming irrational and I tried very hard to snap out of it. I informed the doctor again that I had every intention of taking care of our daughter myself. We wanted her hospitalized as little as possible. At least we all agreed on that. The doctor gave me his telephone number at home and told me several times not to hesitate to call him any time I felt I needed to.

He mentioned remissions. Ninety percent of the time you had a remission, and he seemed quite sure that Mona would have one, too. I felt relieved. Then he explained the medication and its effects.

"We're able to destroy ninety-nine point nine percent of the harmful cells. But we know of no treatment that can destroy them completely. It always returns."

He *had* to tell me "it always returns" just when a little peace was beginning to come into my heart.

And as he turned to leave, he added, "Fine. That'll do for now."

Fine for him! He didn't think twice about saying, "That'll do

for now," and going off with a clear conscience. He thought it was
that simple. From now on, lady, forget your fine dreams. Death is
close by, can't you feel it? You *must* learn to feel it! There's no
other way out. Why let yourself in for more suffering?

But could there be more suffering than this?

Along with all my other chores, every day I went to the hospital, that place where they do everything possible to keep you alive even though they know death is just around the corner. The facilities were clean and the personnel very nice, especially in a case like Mona's, I often thought bitterly, where they knew it wouldn't last forever. The nurses were kind and they quickly became attached to the children. I held only one thing against them: they knew the end of the story too well. And so they showered the children with special attention. It eased their suffering and convinced the parents that the case was hopeless.

Mona was allowed every privilege. We were given a twenty-four hour pass, and we vowed to do everything possible for her. Every morning André drove fifteen miles to spend an hour with Mona. In the afternoon I dropped him off at the school where he taught from one o'clock to seven. I would have just enough time for a couple of games with her, then I had to rush home to meet Francis when the school bus dropped him off. When I was late, he trooped off sadly to a neighbour's house. We spared no effort for our daughter. She had to know that we loved her and wanted to protect her.

I tried in vain to balance my love between my sick daughter and Francis, who was shunted off to the baby-sitter more often than he should have been. But though I tried to convince myself that the arrangement was only temporary, that soon I would be bringing Mona home, and then Francis would have everything he needed, I couldn't help feeling guilty when I saw how sad my son often looked these days.

Mona's doctor warned me not to neglect Francis. "You should

be paying attention to him. After all, he'll be the one who's left . . ."

And, as with every time he reminded me of my daughter's death, my throat grew tight and my heart sank. Wouldn't he ever let me forget, even for a minute? I did what I could, the best way I knew how. I didn't get in the way at the hospital, I tried to make myself useful, I never left Mona's side when she cried. I didn't understand why they were criticizing me for enjoying a few hours with my daughter.

I was proud of myself. I was holding up pretty well. Twenty-four hours at a time — I never stopped repeating it. Why even think of tomorrow? Besides, I was much too busy to spend time licking my wounds. I was planning the move and doing my best to be with Francis. He was asking more and more questions about his sister, and was becoming more and more concerned. To reassure him, we asked permission to take him to play with her one Sunday afternoon. We promised to keep the children in a little room off to the side. It seemed to me that they gave their permission a little too easily.

For the first time in two weeks the family was all together, and it was all André and I could do to hold back our tears as we watched the children greet each other. They didn't know how to show how much they had missed one another, and they hugged each other awkwardly. But after the emotion of the first few minutes, they went back to playing and teasing each other just as they had always done. I had to break up their scuffles from time to time, because Francis could be rough and I was afraid that Mona would tire too quickly.

André and I had grown used to the place; the hospital had become part of our routine. One of us would automatically push the elevator button for the fifth floor. We just naturally turned right towards pediatrics. Even the characteristic hospital smell didn't bother us any more.

One Saturday afternoon, as we opened the door to the ward, we were greeted by the sounds of Mona crying and sobbing. That *was* our daughter, we could never mistake her voice. Our hearts pounding, we rushed to her room and stopped at the threshold. She was in bed, her face stained with tears. A bottle was hanging from a stand above her head and a long red tube was carrying someone else's blood to her veins.

"How long has she been crying like this?" we demanded. It was better to say that than to show our shock. We had never really believed she would need blood.

A nurse was sitting by her bed, keeping an eye on her. "If somebody wasn't always coming in to disturb her, she might feel better."

André got mad. They'd let his daughter cry. Grimly, he went to the desk and spoke to the intern.

"Why didn't you call us? I told you we were available. You were supposed to let us know if something happened."

The doctor tried to explain that they couldn't call every time some little thing changed, but André paid no attention. For him, this was no little change. It was very important if his four-year-old daughter had to have blood. It was hard to get used to seeing a child getting a transfusion. Suddenly she seemed much sicker to us. Like all worried parents, we had a million questions that needed answering.

A pediatrician came in, examined the apparatus and studied Mona carefully. I whispered, "What happened? Has she gotten worse?"

"She needed blood." And in a cold, professional voice, she added, "Try to keep her from scratching her nose. Otherwise she'll start bleeding, which is exactly what we want to avoid."

I hated all these professionals trained to feel and say nothing, but Mona was calling me so I did my best to get a hold of myself. I remembered the effects of the medication. The doctor had warned us, "We are destroying the healthy cells in the blood as well as the harmful ones."

That meant they had to replace her blood. There were so many things to remember. Calmer, we returned to Mona's bedside. She stopped crying and said she had been waiting to see us all morning. For the rest of the day we paid even more attention to her. Live twenty-four hours at a time, I told myself, live in the present. Be strong for her; you owe her that much. You must not let her see that you're sad. You must believe what you're telling her or else she'll sense your uncertainty.

I gathered up my courage and said to Mona, "You see my lamb, they're giving you blood today because you needed it. That way you'll feel a lot better tomorrow."

Mona complained about a funny feeling in her stomach. She said she felt like a thousand little bugs were stinging her all over, especially in her nose. I asked if there was something that could be done, and when they shook their heads, I decided that if I really wanted to do what was best for Mona, I would have to be tough.

"Mona, stop scratching your nose. You heard what the doctor said."

I forgot the long red tube. I forgot that I wanted to be there on that bed and suffer in her place. I told her her favourite story, and with a little more emphasis than usual, I pronounced the last lines: "Then they kissed and lived happily ever after."

The tranfusion took all day. In the evening, a priest who was a friend of the family came to visit. When he saw the child half asleep next to the bag of blood, he blessed her discreetly. Images of death flooded before my eyes. A man on his deathbed, his bones sticking through his waxy skin, a beatific expression on his face because he had been fortunate enough to die blessed by a priest.

I was getting shaky, and the days that followed were less than pleasant. I tried to cheer Mona up, and my mother did the same; we were probably all crowding her too close. In less time than I thought possible, Mona's morale plummeted. She refused to eat. I didn't know what to do.

Then the blood disease specialist happened to witness a scene in Mona's room. My mother was clutching Mona to her like a newborn who wouldn't take the breast. Mona had refused to eat supper and her grandmother was stroking her head. What more can you do for a doomed child?

The specialist said, "There's no reason why Mona should be so listless. I checked her file. Since the transfusion, her hemoglobin has been normal. You shouldn't coddle her too much, you know."

I realized I hadn't kept my word. Maternal instinct and pity had made me lose my grip and I had been communicating my own sadness to Mona. I had been spoiling her precious days.

All that would change, I promised myself. From now on, everyone who came to visit would see that I had changed. For Mona's sake, I would steel myself against the outside world.

One afternoon, surrounded by piles of boxes packed for moving, as I was considering the battery of medical statistics and the pros and cons of my new way of looking at things, there was a knock on the door. Like any proper hostess, I forgot all about my preoccupations and welcomed a cousin of mine who had come calling.

She had brought a casserole. "You must not feel much like cooking in the situation you're in."

I didn't need anyone reminding me about my situation, but I offered her the obligatory cup of coffee, plus cookies for her kids. Of course the toy box was opened to them too. The two boys, three and four years old, went at the toys with gusto and soon everything they could get their hands on was spread around the room.

While the children played, my cousin got around to the real reason for her visit. She had done some investigating of her own into leukemia. A friend of hers, who happened to be a lab technician, had heard of a case just like Mona's and had told her all about the disease. Full of good intentions, my cousin cheerfully shared her information with me. "If you only knew how upset I was when I heard. I could hardly go on, I didn't know what to think. . . ."

I shifted uncomfortably. What could I say? Was I supposed to console *her*? She said she had done a little arithmetic, and if Mona survived another couple of years, her own kids would be very affected by her death.

"They'll be five and six by then. At that age, kids understand a lot."

I stirred my coffee; I couldn't believe my ears, let alone bring myself to look at her. Was I hearing right? Was she asking for *her* children to be spared?

"They try not to make it look so bad," she went on, "talking about two years and all. A lot of kids who have leukemia don't even last that long."

Completely dumbfounded, I stammered out a few words. I never expected anything like this! No sooner had I emerged from the depths of despair than she was pushing me down again. To hide my feelings, I began to talk, say the first thing that came into my head, anything to shut her up.

"I'll have to get a new bed for Mona. Her old bed won't fit in the new kids' room. I want to try a different set-up with two little beds without backboards. I'll arrange them like this."

And I showed her what I was planning to do, when she interrupted, "Be reasonable. You shouldn't buy a new bed for Mona. It's not worth it. Hold onto your money, you'll need it."

I was stunned. If I had a sick dog, I'd still buy him food for the next week. I thought of the price of caskets. My cousin advised me to face reality.

"I pray that it doesn't drag on too long. I'm sure it'll be better if it's over soon."

I pulled myself from the wreckage of my hopes and managed to blurt out that she should mind her own business and keep her prayers to herself. I didn't know what else I said but I must have been reasonably polite, since she didn't leave until she had drained her cup of coffee, without noticing the devastating effect she had had on me. After all, I hadn't cried. Nobody seemed to realize that my tears had long since run dry.

My heart in turmoil, I paced through the kitchen and living room. I stumbled over the boxes piled on the floor. I went from one window to the next, from the telephone to the bathroom. From hatred to fear. From my dreams for a new children's room to the funeral parlour.

In the midst of all this, I spotted my son's bus bringing him back from school. It never failed: every time one of my children was around, I regained my self-control.

"Hi there, young man! How was school today?"

"Hi, Mom!"

I made him his favourite snack. Then I took out the telephone book and turned to the Yellow Pages under Furniture. I dialed the number.

"May I help you?"

"I'm interested in buying a bed."

That evening in our bedroom, I told my husband about everything that was seething inside me. I got more wound up as I talked, and practically shouted at him, "What did *I* do to *her*? She actually dared tell me that she would pray for Mona to die as soon as possible. Just wait till she tells me *her* mother is sick. I'll say now isn't that too bad? I hope she won't hang around for too long. Taking care of sick people gets to be a drag."

I went on and on, but when I stopped to catch my breath, André finally got a word in.

"Hold on! Don't take everything she says so seriously."

But I continued, "It's as if she wants me to get rid of her faster so her little dears won't suffer."

"You're exaggerating and you know it."

"And to top it all off, she told me not to buy a new bed for Mona. She told me to keep the money to buy a . . ."

"Money means a lot to her. I'm sure she only wanted to help."

"Go ahead, defend her!"

And after I blurted out those words we fell asleep, the gulf widening between us.

W e had a call from the intern whom my husband had bawled out for not having told us about the transfusion. Today, with more than a hint of irony, he informed us that Mona would be changing rooms. Her treatment was destroying her white blood cells, the ones that fight infection. To make her less vulnerable to germs and viruses, they planned to put her in a room away from the other children.

They found a room-mate for Mona, a six-year-old girl who was in the hospital for frequent nose bleeds. When she arrived there, she looked like a corpse. She was frail and had big sad eyes. Her parents lived far away and they made the long trip to see her two or three times a week.

Danielle and Mona became good friends, and in the evenings we now had another player for our games. The two girls used the intercom to order popsicles and their favourite fruit juices. They encouraged each other to take their pills. They had a television just for themselves and they shared their secrets. Their room smelled of antiseptic even more than the other rooms, but the atmosphere was a lot warmer. All the same, Danielle rarely smiled and never laughed.

Mona left her room once a day to go to the pay phone. She climbed onto a chair, put a dime in the slot and dialed the number that her father had written on a piece of paper for her. A few seconds later, the phone would ring in our kitchen and she would describe what she had done with Danielle that morning. She talked to Mommy, Dad, her brother, and she always signed off with kisses for everyone.

For the hundredth time, she would ask, "What time are you going to come see me?"

And we promised her that when the little hand was on the seven and the big hand on the twelve, we'd be there.

One day a nurse spotted Mona returning to her room. "What are you doing out here? You're supposed to be in your room."

But Mona was smiling so happily that the nurse closed her eyes to the infraction and forgot about the few germs Mona had encountered in the hallway.

"The nurse doesn't want to put my hair in pigtails any more," Mona said.

"Why not?"

"I don't know. She's not allowed to."

For a moment we forgot about our exuberant daughter bouncing on the bed and went to have a chat with Danielle's parents. They were sitting at her bedside. Danielle's nose had bled all day, and she was lying in bed with cotton in her nostrils. Her big eyes were the only sign of life in her face. Her mother looked worn out. She had four other children and so much to do. Her husband had a job that took him out of town, and he had to travel a great deal. Poor Danielle! Her parents told us how busy and exhausted they were. And Danielle was just one more burden.

I didn't want to get caught up in their sadness, so I only half listened as Danielle's mother talked on. I promised myself to be kind to this frail child and give her the kind of physical affection that she obviously wasn't used to getting. I made a mental note to wish Danielle sweet dreams too when I left Mona for the night, and after I kissed Mona and held her in my arms, I ran my hand over Danielle's forehead. I felt her shrink back. Danielle's mother had come to the end of her story and said, "The doctors thought Danielle had the same thing your daughter has. Now they're not so sure."

I was stunned. How could she even compare the two? Mona couldn't be as sick as that pitiful little girl!

Two months later I heard Danielle had died. It came as no surprise, but when it happened, I was forced to listen to words I didn't want to hear. Danielle's mother attacked the doctors. What else can you do when your world falls apart? She said they had released her daughter from the hospital too soon, and that she had caught some virus. It wasn't her fault that she had died. She had done everything in her power to save her, but the fever had been too strong. They'd even done a tracheotomy in the hospital. Then Danielle's mother calmed down and said in a resigned voice, "Something like this happened in my husband's family. Someone's blood didn't have enough platelets."

I fought to keep from being dragged down by her despair. What would I have done if it had been me? And why did it have to be her?

Later I asked Mona, "Do you remember Danielle?" I spoke of her in the past tense. "She was nice, wasn't she?"

Mona nodded her head . . . and her eyes were filled with vivid memories. I never had the heart to mention Danielle again.

The telephone was ringing.

"I can hear it but I can't find it."

"It's there, under that heap of clothes."

"Hello?"

"Hi! It's me, Elida."

Elida was Roger's wife, my husband's brother. They lived in New York. When she heard that her niece was sick, she had looked into special clinics. She talked to me encouragingly about remissions, about treatments similar to Mona's, about all the research that was taking place, and about the progress that had been made over the years.

"If you need anything, please call us. We'd like to help."

I was grateful. Her voice was positive and her words helped me to keep up the struggle. I combed my mop of hair and started packing again, my heart a bit lighter. I thought of everyone who had offered to help us, including a girlfriend of mine who was busy cleaning the new apartment, and my parents who had given us the living-room rug. Think of it as your Christmas present, they had told us. I was a little embarrassed by such a fine gift, and I wondered when I would ever be able to express my gratitude in a more material way. I thanked God for having given me an iron constitution. I was on the run morning, noon and night, but holding up fine all the same. I had enough energy for the hospital, both apartments and my son, too.

But André was starting to get on my nerves. He felt left out; people had forgotten all about him. But this was no time to get moody. He could do what I did: it was called crisis management, one step at a time. I was pressed for time and his sensitive nature suffered. He didn't like being at the mercy of others: he was too proud for that. He wanted to be his family's provider, and other people were starting to take his place. He wanted to buy Mona some slippers, but one of her aunts had already taken care of it. He wanted to give me the house of my dreams, but he didn't have enough money. He couldn't get me a cleaning lady, so all my friends had to come and help. He was frustrated by his own failings which had suddenly become all too evident.

I consoled myself by remembering what a good father he was. He was the one who took the children for walks in the woods, teaching them about nature. And Francis could always count on him to listen to his first-grade adventures.

And he was the one who had convinced Mona to take her pills after she had refused to take them. Having exhausted all the tricks of the trade, the nurse was finally losing patience and was ready to use pure force.

"Let me give it a try," André said.

Away from everyone else, off in the washroom, he explained to Mona how you could swallow pills without having to taste them. All you had to do was put them at the back of your tongue. She stopped crying and listened to him. She would try, just for Dad. And as he left, he said to the nurse, "From now on, Mona will take her pills without a fuss."

Mona proudly listened to her father make the announcement. She wasn't going to disappoint him.

But right now we were moving, and I didn't need a loving and sensitive husband, I needed a strong man. Yesterday, without even asking me, he had agreed to take Mona home on the very day of our move. It was all I needed! He couldn't wait one more day after the doctor had given him the good news. "On Wednesday, you can take her home."

He agreed because he knew how eager Mona was to get out of the hospital, and he knew that I would get along somehow. He promised to be at the nursing station at three o'clock to take Mona home. I was furious at him for having made all the arrangements without asking me. The apartment would never be ready for her.

It was seven o'clock in the morning and I was running from room to room, doing the last bits of packing up, in between a few bites of breakfast. Francis left for school at eight-thirty, leaving me a half hour to put away the rest of the dishes. The truck would be coming soon for the furniture.

"Where should I put this stuff?" André asked me.

"How should I know!"

He looked me straight in the eye. "Calm down, all right?"

I did, but not as much as he would have liked. I was afraid of losing momentum if I calmed down too much; I'd be just like he was. André was so cool that he ended up not doing anything much. At every step of the way, he would ask me what he should do next. But my mind was on a thousand different things, and I replied sarcastically. Finally, help arrived: my mother and a neighbour.

"He's supposed to get Mona at three o'clock," I told them.

"It doesn't make sense," my mother objected. "Postpone it. We'll never be finished by then."

"It's too late now, I've tried. He says the doctors have to see him to explain how to give the medication. Besides, Mona would be too disappointed. We'll just have to be ready for her by supper-time. We'll start with the kids' room, the cupboards and the closets. We'll do the kitchen shelves afterwards. The men will take care of the big pieces of furniture. They'll put in the stove, the fridge and the washing machine."

And the race against time began.

I was so preoccupied that I even forgot my daughter was sick. Only one thing mattered: we had to be finished by suppertime.

With that thought in mind, we only stopped once, for lunch, and I didn't even taste the food. My back hurt from bending over so much. I washed out the drawers and shelves, and as I drank a cup of coffee, I glanced at my reddened hands. One o'clock already. I took a deep breath and got back to work.

There I was, bent over a box of sheets, my hair flying every which way. André was hanging around holding a screwdriver. I knew what he was thinking: he didn't like the harassed look on my face. He didn't want me looking like a cleaning lady. I had always secretly resented him for being able to do things for pleasure, while I ended up doing them out of duty. But this was no time for pleasure. It wasn't my fault that things had turned out this way, and it was about time that my Lord and Master took his nose out of his books and started facing reality. Somebody had to do the job and right now it was me, the woman he chose to share his life with, who had to do it. It took him three tries before he was able to put Mona's bed together. He kept trying to put the wrong pieces together. I saw he was doing it wrong, but I didn't dare tell him. All I said was, "Don't go and get Mona until you've finished setting up her room."

I pitied him, and was mad at him at the same time. But then somebody shouted, "Where do you want this table," and I was forced to forget André and carry on. Putting things away, dusting them, hanging the curtains. At three o'clock, completely exhausted, I wanted to drop into a chair, but they were all piled high with things. There was no choice but to go on setting up the furniture, arranging the kitchen, cleaning off the chairs, carrying the boxes we wouldn't have time to empty into André's office and closing the door on the whole mess. He had already left. Soon he'd be back with Mona.

I wanted to prepare myself mentally and catch my breath. But the house wasn't ready. I was worried about how Mona would react to the new place. She had left for the hospital almost three weeks ago, and she would be coming home to a new house, without having said goodbye to the old one.

I phoned the store and ordered some groceries. I was slowing down and starting to get frazzled. Francis came back from school and this made me twice as nervous. I had to start thinking about supper, even though I just felt like throwing up. I started looking for my dishes but couldn't find a thing.

Frustrated, I asked my mother, "Where did you hide the pots?"

My mother had worked hard to arrange the cupboards as best she could so I would have fewer boxes to empty. She knew I would soon have my hands full, so she had put away as many things as possible without asking if they were in the right place. Despite my irritation, her voice was full of compassion.

"You can reorganize your cupboards the way you like later, when you have more time."

Everybody who had helped us slumped into chairs. At least two of them planned to stay for supper. I had to dredge up the strength to make something to eat. I'd just gotten started when André came in with Mona in his arms. She was so pale that I shivered. It seemed to me that she looked a lot worse than when she had first gone to the hospital. I hadn't had the chance to go and see her for the last two days, and I was struck by how dreadful she looked.

"Hello there, big girl."

As I kissed her and took off her coat, I couldn't help noticing how pale her little hands were. All those inquiring eyes made her uncomfortable, and I wished her homecoming could have taken place with just the family there. Mona stayed close to her father as he showed her her new room. She wanted to sit on his lap. I was busy making supper, but I still kept an eye on her. She wasn't smiling like she used to. She must have felt as though she was on display. If only all those people weren't watching her! I knew too well what they were thinking; they were wondering how long she was going to last.

Mona did look much weaker. She had trouble walking, as if her body was too heavy for her legs. We served her first and she picked at her food.

After supper was over the conversation dragged. If only I could be alone with Mona! But I didn't know how to ask someone I loved to leave. I grasped for the right words: Mother, please, you've helped enough as it is. Go now . . . But I couldn't say it. I wanted to be alone with Mona, but at the same time I was afraid to. I wanted my mother to leave and stay at the same time. So I cleared the table instead, even though every bone in my body was aching.

When they finally left, I kissed my mother good-bye and closed the door behind her. I had been on the go for weeks, but tonight I thought I had reached my limit. Yet somehow I was going to have to find the energy to breathe some life into this new house and give some to every member of my family. But I felt so empty, I only wanted to run from it all. Why was it up to me to provide the life here? Why didn't André do it?

He was busy fixing the television. In spite of everything, it seemed to be up to me as a woman to breathe life into these four walls that I hadn't even chosen, with a sick child, a tense husband

and a worried son. Everyone was counting on me. It was "Mommy" this and "Mommy" that, like fledglings in a nest.

It was already time to put the kids to bed. I intended to follow the hospital schedule because it would be easier on Mona. I took care of the children and ignored André. I couldn't start talking to him: I had too much to say and I was too tired to say it.

I kissed the children goodnight and made sure to whisper to Francis that I loved him just as much, even if I was looking after Mona a little more. That night, I fell asleep at my husband's side, but I was miles away from him. The words whirled around in my head: help me, I need you! I know you need help too. But you don't understand, you're so stubborn! I had thought it was our love that kept us together. But I wasn't sure anymore, I was so tired. And I fell asleep before I could find the words that would bring us together again.

Part II

I did my best to be a good nurse. I gave Mona her medication at the right time, I bathed her and catered to her needs. But I was having trouble learning to live with my daughter again; she had changed so much. I told myself that it would take her a little time to get used to being home after the hospital. Mona didn't seem to know which way to turn. She sat motionless for hours on end. Between pill-time and meal-time — I prepared each meal carefully so it would contain the right vitamins and protein — I would play with her, but nothing held her interest. If I did manage to hold her attention, she always wanted to win whatever game we were playing. Despite my good intentions, I couldn't lose every time. Mona lost patience quickly.

"My legs hurt! They hurt, Mommy, they hurt!" she would cry.

And I would run to get the Absorbine to rub her with. When Mona wanted a rub-down, she had to have one right away. Massages eased her pain, so I massaged her. If she refused to get dressed after her morning bath, then I put her pyjamas back on. Dressed like that, she really did look sick. She would sit in the big armchair and stare out the window.

Mona had been back home only a few days, but I was already at my wits' end. She was in terrible shape. I called the doctor. I was so worried that he told me to bring her to the hospital so he could take a blood sample. I realized that he was just trying to calm me down, and I was berating myself for making Mona undergo a needless blood test when the doctor returned with the results.

"The platelet count is two thousand."

"But that's not enough! It should be two hundred thousand, shouldn't it?"

He nodded. "We can't do anything today. The next treatment is in three days. We'll have to be patient and wait for it to take effect."

Mona was tired and depressed. To cheer her up, the doctor offered to buy her some candy, and we went down to the tuck shop. Mona didn't know what she wanted. The doctor was in a hurry, and I urged her to make up her mind.

"Here, take this one."

"No, I want the other one." And she pointed at one thing after another.

After she refused all my suggestions, I picked out something I thought she would like. Getting more and more irritated, she finally threw herself on the floor and went into a tantrum. I'd never seen her like that; I was at an absolute loss. She used to be such a good-natured child. As I tried to soothe her, I went from fear to anger, and then to compassion. I would start crying pretty soon myself if she didn't stop. I carried her out of the shop. She twisted and turned in my arms. I was out of breath.

"I've never seen her act like this," I said to the doctor despairingly.

"It must be the result of the medication."

They had had her in their care for three weeks, and so far the effects of the treatments had been negative. But I didn't dare remind him of that — he might run out of ways of keeping my hopes up.

As if to share my distress, he added, "Don't hesitate to call me whenever you need to." Comforted in some small way by the fact that he was so ready to help, I headed home, determined to be patient. Patience was a virtue I lacked. Patience with my kids, with my husband, with life in general. I wanted too much of everything, I wanted everything to come at once. I had to learn how to wait. And I *would* learn.

André's big brother had had a fight with his wife and he had come up from New York. He had driven all day and hadn't slept the night before.

"Hi! Where's Elida?"

"She didn't come."

"What's the matter? You two just got married!"

"She doesn't know I'm here and I don't want to tell her. If you tell her, I don't want her to know that I know."

"Look, my life is complicated enough as it is. Do you want me to tell her you're here or not?"

"No, don't tell her."

Since I had enough on my mind without worrying about other people's problems, I decided just to treat him like an ordinary guest. André and Big Rog started in on the beer and then they decided to go downtown to drink in peace while I, of course, stayed behind with the kids.

"That's right, you two go and have a good chat."

André realized it was better not to try and kiss me. They didn't tell me where they were going, but just took off, guiltily. I wiped away a tear at the unfairness of it all, then I got down to the business of cooking another meal. Mona was watching me and I tried to act nonchalant, but I couldn't help mashing the potatoes with a little extra vigour.

The men came home late for supper, of course, feeling no pain. They said the most banal things to each other, then broke up laughing like a couple of idiots. Suddenly, turning serious, André held up Mona's hands. "Look how white they are."

The two brothers exchanged a glance. A glance I caught just as

I was bringing them their supper. And the look in their eyes made me set their plates down a little more gently.

That evening I felt sociable enough to have visitors. Some friends came over, bringing beer. Mona was in bed asleep. Finally I could pour myself a drink and try to laugh along with the others.

They were all laughing about Roger who had come up to Canada with his dog instead of his wife.

"He's a lot more obedient," Roger joked.

I didn't think he was very funny, but I tried my best to find something to be happy about. Wasn't laughter better than tears? So I raised my glass and laughed at their silly jokes and tried to forget my problems. After all, none of this was their fault. And I liked having a good time, too.

Then Mona woke up, and everyone crowded around her. "Poor little girl," they all said.

It was as if someone had dropped a bomb on the party. Our guests suddenly became very subdued. They abruptly turned down the snack I offered them and left, carrying their empty case of beer. Holding Mona in my arms, I thanked them for coming, wondering what had changed their mood so quickly. I looked at my daughter. Her face was a little puffy, the way you look when you just wake up. Well, maybe a little more than usual. She wanted to go pee.

In the harsh light of the bathroom, I could see Mona's face more clearly. I saw her every day, but I hadn't noticed how swollen she had become. I lowered the one-piece pyjama she wore so an elastic wouldn't dig into her skin. As I set her on the toilet, I saw how big her stomach was. I examined her carefully, as if I had never really seen her before. I raised her little arms and made her turn around, holding my breath every time I saw her from a different angle. My child was becoming deformed before my very eyes. Her body was swollen, her face was fat, and a sort of hump was forming on the back of her neck. Her limbs were thin, and she was as white as a ghost. My knees trembled. She tried to catch my eye, and I quickly regained my composure.

Very deliberately — because I felt like running away — I carried her back to bed.

"Good night, my love."

I left her room as quickly as possible. Didn't anyone else see how she had changed? Was I the first? No. I was the last.

"I did notice," André said.

"You didn't say anything to me."

"Why should I? You'd see it soon enough."

Every mother wants to believe that her child is beautiful, and I was no exception.

"She was always so beautiful. Maybe she was a little chubby, but now. . . ." My words were lost in sobs. I had to know what to expect — right away.

"I'm going to call the doctor."

"Don't disturb him. What difference will one night make?"

Reluctantly, I ended up giving in to his cold reasoning. I withdrew into myself and locked myself in my room. As for André, he expressed his pain by writing a long poem in which Mona's life was in danger.

"Doctor, Mona is all swollen."

"That's the effect of the cortisone. As soon as she stops taking it, the swelling will subside."

That was all I wanted to know. If I had to live with a child with swollen cheeks and a fat stomach, well then, I'd live with it. It wasn't the end of the world.

I needed time. If it had been for sale, I would have bought some. In twenty-four hour lots. I had so many things to learn. As a distraction from all the sickness and its ugliness I began decorating our new house. That helped a lot. So did a good cry, which came courtesy of my mother-in-law.

As you might expect, she found out that "her" Roger was staying at our place, and she took all her bile out on me.

"Why didn't you call? You can't imagine how his poor wife has been suffering. She's been looking for him for the last forty-eight hours. Surely a phone call wouldn't have been too much to ask."

My dear mother-in-law insisted that I do something for the newlyweds, that I be more sensitive to their little spats.

But I'd been taking it on all sides long enough, and I wasn't about to put up with anything from my mother-in-law. I felt like shouting back, "Your grand-daughter is swelling up like a balloon, and what do you care? Anyway, I hate your two sons. They expect to be waited on hand and foot, and it's your fault that they turned out that way." But of course I didn't say anything like that. I just handed the phone over to Roger.

In my room, I pounded my fists into my pillow. They were all a bunch of cannibals, and I was too easy a target for them. Why the hell hadn't I ever learned to fight back? Why had my mother always kept me from jumping into the fray? But that was against the rules: I was encouraged to be obedient and good, whatever that meant.

My thoughts wandered back to my childhood and I felt myself teetering on the edge of depression. All I wanted was a home for my daughter — a happy home, although I didn't know what those words meant any more. I felt as if everything was going to fly apart, unravel, break into a thousand pieces. I tried to breathe more slowly to regain control of my panicked body. My sobs had put my stomach in knots. I couldn't lose my grip on things. No use destroying myself now. Who would look after Mona if I made myself sick? And that thought helped dissolve the lump in my throat and lift the weight from my heart.

As I watered my withering coleus, I realized that I had been neglecting my plants. I put them in front of the sunniest window. There wasn't much sun in November, but at least they could soak up the last few rays. Then I had a brilliant idea. A dog might be a way of breathing a little happiness and life into this house.

Mona and I went to pick out a new puppy. She carried it like a doll, all wrapped up in a blanket. Kiki became Mona's playmate and confidant, and the two were devoted to one another. Despite his high spirits, he quietly let himself be petted for hours at a time. He would be the patient when Mona decided to play doctor, the pupil when she wanted to play teacher. When she was too sick to play, he waited patiently by her side until she felt better again.

To lengthen my daughter's life, once a week they had to inject some strong medicine into her veins. But Mona was resisting. She wouldn't have any part of this "poison," as she called it. She didn't like shots.

Everything possible was done to make her ordeal less painful. We rarely had to wait. As soon as we walked in, Mona's favourite doctor greeted us. A nurse was called who not only possessed the gift of divine patience, but was also very skilled at giving shots to young children. Very gently, without a shred of impatience, she explained over and over to Mona what she was about to do. But poor Mona would begin to cry at the very sight of the needle and syringe.

"Come now, I'm just going to give you one little shot."

I wished I could get a hundred shots rather than have to see my daughter suffer through one! The nurse said, "You're lucky. I'm going to do it all with the same shot. I'm going to take some blood and put in an I.V. while I wait for the results. We'll just use the same tube to give you your medicine. Now give me your hand, I see a nice vein right there on top. . . ."

But as soon as she came near, Mona started screaming again. She was bathed in sweat. I tried to calm her down, and for the hundredth time, I told her, "Put out your hand, kitten, they're doing this to make you healthy again."

And in my ears I heard the doctor's voice echo: *this disease has no cure.*

Finally I couldn't be convincing any more, so I left. The nurse said, "Don't worry, I'll wait until she gives me her hand all by herself."

I went out to gather my courage. Mona would be undergoing these treatments for several weeks, and I didn't think I could go through this torture session every time. I trusted the medical team that had chosen the treatment; now I would have to put my faith in that highly potent solution they were injecting into my daughter's veins. I pictured the medication doing battle against the harmful cells it would meet on its path.

Calmer now, I returned to Mona's room. Tearfully, Mona begged me to take her home: her own struggling had exhausted her.

In my most authoritarian tone I told her, "Mona, enough's enough! Put out your hand and let's get it over with. Look, I brought you a puppet. We can play with it while they give you the I.V."

And finally the needle was put into her little hand and blood was taken to the laboratory.

"See, it's not so bad. You were very brave, darling."

The two nurses left, visibly relieved. Mona let out a few final sobs which I pretended not to hear. I launched into a story about the puppet. The doctor returned with his little vials for the injection.

"I'll go get the results from the lab to save us some time," he said.

"Good idea. My puppet is tired. He's run out of things to say to Mona."

50

Through half-closed eyes, she examined the puppet lying flat on its stomach, its neck bent like a hanged man. She smiled. It was the finest reward she could have given me, and I forgot my weariness.

The results were still bad. As he mixed his potions, the doctor explained that he wouldn't order another transfusion as long as the hemoglobin stayed above six. Her current level was seven point five, but the normal count was twelve. He washed the vein after the injection by putting the I.V. back for a few minutes. He gave Mona a big kiss and a quarter. She agreed to go straight home, too tired even to spend the money.

Mona listened to me tell her father about our adventures at the hospital. "It's no good tiring her out like that every time," I concluded.

Mona glanced from my face to her father's face. What had she done wrong to make us so worried about her?

"Climb aboard," André said to her.

And she clambered onto his lap, happy that he was his old self again.

"Show me your shot."

She showed him the little hole. And he explained to her, a four-year-old girl, that if she believed with all her heart that a little shot like that wouldn't hurt, then she wouldn't feel a thing.

"It's really true. You won't feel anything at all if you set your mind to it."

Just before the next injection, he told her about the power of positive thinking, which he called "what happens when you think real, real hard."

"Remember," he told her, "you have to think very hard that it won't hurt."

Imagine, a four-year-old child! She believed what her Daddy said like it was gospel. If he said it, it *must* be true.

And she would do it, just for him.

When the nurse came in for the injection, Mona closed her eyes and concentrated very hard on what her father had said. She walked out, head held high in triumph. It hadn't hurt a bit and she didn't even cry. Her Dad would be very proud of her. We owed ourselves a little reward from the hospital cafeteria.

"What do you feel like eating?"

"A hot dog."

"But it will make you swell up even more, and besides, it's not good for you. Why don't you have something else?"

She had just made a very big effort and here I was already asking her to make another. She looked so disappointed that I quickly said to the woman behind the counter, "Two hot dogs, please."

The four walls of my house were closing in on me. In the past, I had gotten used to working part time and meeting people. Now I was suffocating at home with my little patient; I wanted to get out into the world again. André should have been able to realize that. I decided to take Mona and go and see my family. The doctor agreed; a change of scene wouldn't do Mona any harm. A friend offered to look after Francis after school and give him his dinner.

"Let me go, I really need to get away," I told André.

But he didn't understand the first thing about my needs. He said he was worried about Francis, but I sensed that he was more worried about himself. I knew he was disappointed that I felt I had to travel a hundred miles to find the support that I was looking for, but I had prepared myself for the trip and I was going to go ahead with it, no matter what.

My parents welcomed us with open arms, and the atmosphere was warm and homey. Everyone was there for dinner, even my married brother. They served a special menu, all of Mona's favourite foods.

Sitting around the table, we chatted about one thing and another. Everyone teased Mona the way they had always done, but it was obvious from the looks on their faces how much she had changed. Suddenly I was sorry that my younger brothers had to see all this, and I was touched by how hard they tried to behave naturally.

There was another leukemia case in the town where my parents lived, and they set up a meeting between the other mother and myself. We spoke of our common grief as if we had known each other for years. Her daughter had had leukemia for over three years. It had been a tough time. Besides her daughter's illness, she had had to deal with her husband's depression. He hadn't been able to cope and had had a breakdown. Her daughter had been in remission for the last three years. I hung on every word she said, and wondered why her child had lasted that long. If hers had, why not mine? I was only asking for a few more months.

"Hasn't she been sick since then?" I asked.

"No. She has her treatments, that's all. Just a cold once in a while."

Her eyes shone as she spoke of how devoted she and her husband were to their daughter, and she described all kinds of details about her little girl — the clever things she said, how sweet she was.

This woman, all five-feet-seven of her, radiated so much energy that it shone through her words. She had enough strength for two. She had hidden everything from her other two children — and sought out a private place when she had to cry. If she heard of someone succumbing to leukemia, she increased her own efforts. She would rouse her husband into action. "Come on, let's go out tonight," she'd urge him.

They didn't stand there paralyzed with fear, just because it might be their turn next time.

We compared treatments. They had already improved. Who knew, researchers might find better ones still. The prospect gave me new hope. My new friend did admit that she dreaded the onset of adolescence, for that was a dangerous time.

"If she has to die," she said, "I'd rather she die young so she won't have to be too aware of what's happening to her."

Those were the last words I wanted to hear. To lessen their sting, I kept clinging to the thought of a three-year remission. I would have settled for that any day! I could practically taste those years. I could already see my daughter with three more years on this earth, three good years, and by the time they had elapsed, the geniuses of medical science would have discovered some extraordinary cure.

But a few days later, in the doctor's office, my fine dream was shattered.

"No two cases are alike," the doctor warned me. "A three-year remission is very rare indeed. It's the only one we've ever seen in the area."

Before leaving my family, still under the influence of the woman's encouraging words, I went to see a favourite aunt of mine. Something was bothering me, and before long my aunt guessed what I wanted to talk about.

"Why is it always the wife who has to stay home when the children are sick? Who says that's the way it has to be?"

The burden was growing too heavy. I envied my husband: he left every morning and his mind was on something else when he was teaching. But circumstances had forced me back to my four walls. Of course I loved Mona, but my maternal love was encroaching on my own sense of freedom. I realized that the family home run by the woman was ancient history and that we had to create a new kind of home. But why did I have to do it? The constant effort was wearing me out.

"Why does the wife have to do everything?"

"When it comes to the house, my girl, the woman keeps things going. She keeps it alive."

"Not all by herself."

"No, but if she gives up, then it's bound to fall apart."

"If you ask me, you're putting too much responsibility on the woman."

"Have you ever heard of a good home where the woman has left?"

"No. I guess you're right."

"I'm afraid I am. Now go back and be brave."

And I left her, full of good intentions, ready to make my home live again and be happy as well. It might not be easy, but I'd find a way. As we drove back, I reminded Mona of all the fun we had had that day.

"You're lucky to have such nice grandparents."

"I'm hungry, Mom."

"Already? You're just like a pregnant woman."

"What's a pregnant woman?"

"A mother who's going to have a baby. Sometimes pregnant women absolutely have to have certain things, like special things to eat. But only those who are compensating — but I think that's a little over your head."

We found a little country restaurant. The son was serving at the counter with his mother. He gave Mona a long look and finally said, "She's awfully pale, that girl. Are you sure she's not sick?"

Mona waited to see how I would react.

"Come on, we'll eat in the car."

I ran from the boy who had spoken his mind too easily. I looked at Mona: he had spoken the truth.

I had wanted to keep my spirits up for our return home so André would know that the trip hadn't been in vain, but my heart grew heavy as the sun set. As I drove the Oldsmobile, I looked at the November sky pierced with wide violet stripes. The villagers had built their cemetery much too close to the highway for my taste.

It snowed a little one morning and everything was covered in a white blanket. I rose with a light heart. As usual, the first thing I did was to go and see Mona. She was still in bed.

"Sleep well?"

I noticed that there were hairs on her pillow. But I was so eager to show her how beautiful and white everything was outside that I didn't spend much time thinking about it. After we admired the fresh snow, we sat down for a good breakfast. Mona was wearing her yellow bathrobe. Her hair was very black, and as I served her an egg I saw that there were hundreds of hairs lying on the yellow fabric.

"How come you're not eating breakfast, Mommy?"

I glanced at my watch. It was too late to catch the doctor at home and too soon to contact him at the hospital. I drank a mouthful of coffee and looked at Mona's hair. I'd brush it later. It must be like after an anesthetic, when your hair falls out easily. Or else the medication — it was so strong. I would let Mona take her time and have a good breakfast. First I would give her a bath, and then I would comb her hair.

After I had finished wiping her feet, I started brushing, and a big clump of hair came out at the first stroke. I took the comb and ran it very lightly along the side of her head. It turned black with hair. Not her hair too! It was bad enough that she was pale, swollen and fat. I stroked the strands of hair tenderly, almost wanting to glue them back onto her head.

"What's wrong with my hair?" she asked.

"The pills must be doing that to you, darling."

Then I remembered a lady who had told me at the beginning

to have a photographer take Mona's picture. "Your daughter is going to change a lot. You should take her picture now."

So this was what she meant! Of course I hadn't believed her grim predictions, but now I had to face the facts. My daughter would become unrecognizable. To hide my face from Mona, I bent down to pick up the hair that had fallen to the floor. I took a long time, long enough to wipe the fear and disbelief from my face. I threw her hair into the garbage. More and more hair, all in the garbage. After all, it was nothing more than female vanity.

I called the woman whose daughter had been in remission for three years.

"Did yours lose her hair?"

"No. She had long hair and I didn't even have to cut it. I heard that it's . . . it's only toward the end that they lose their hair."

What was she talking about? Toward the end! Was she such an authority? I was angry with myself for having called her. Why was I in such a hurry to know everything right away? I fought off the desire to call the doctor. What could he possibly tell me? We had an appointment tomorrow. I wouldn't bother him now over a few hairs. So I waited; all day long I waited and picked up hair. Wherever Mona went, she left a trail behind. At mealtime, I made sure that none fell into other people's plates.

I wanted to talk to someone about it, but I knew that nobody else could go through this for me. People would make useless comments, they would pity me, and I'd end up wasting my energy.

That day I dug deep into myself. I realized that what hurt me the most was that I could no longer hide what I was feeling. Everybody would know. Suddenly I had an idea. If Mona didn't have natural hair, there was always the artificial kind: she would wear a wig.

The next day I asked the doctor, "Will Mona really lose all her hair?"

Gravely, he nodded. I pictured my daughter without a hair on her head and I wanted to protest, but Mona was sitting on my lap. Instead, I calmly discussed getting a wig.

"It's a good idea," he said. "Don't wait too long."

I took the money we had saved for heating oil and went off in search of a wig for a four-year-old child. Since I had to spend money, I might as well have some fun. I tried on wigs in all the colours of the rainbow and Mona smiled as she watched me turn blonde, red-head, with short or long hair. But it was impossible to find anything her size. The sales staff wasn't convinced we were serious, and they did little to help. In the end, someone gave us the name of a woman who could adjust wigs.

I breathed down the poor woman's neck. It had to be ready soon. She promised she'd have it for us in two days.

"Hold onto your hair for another couple of days, all right, Mo?"

She smiled, very excited about getting to wear a wig like a grown-up.

It was Halloween.

"Come on, Mona! Let's go trick-or-treating!"

I insisted that Mona be part of the festivities, not because it might be her last, but because I wanted her to have a little fun. She was thrilled to be able to put on her little mask and go knocking on the neighbours' doors while I waited in the shadows, ready to carry her if she didn't feel strong enough to walk. Her legs were giving her so much pain.

"Francis, go to the Tremblays with her, all right? And wait for her, you're going too fast!"

I was glad to see the children smiling. The only thing that stood between us and happiness were the sad looks on other people's faces. They couldn't seem to get over the way Mona had changed. But I thanked them quickly and avoided any dead-end conversations.

Mona had been receiving treatments for five weeks, and life carried on. I couldn't bear to see the looks on people's faces when they stared at Mona's bald head, so I went all out to fix the wig to make it look as real as possible. You had to keep up appearances. When we went to the hospital, I had Mona put on her wig and I put a little rouge on her pale cheeks. She always promised not to take the wig off if she got too hot, but as soon as we got to the cafeteria — we always rewarded ourselves with a little snack after the injection — the heat got too much for her and she pulled off her wig just like a hat. The illusion ended up landing on a chair.

I could only smile at my failure to camouflage the truth. All around I heard gasps of shock and pity.

"Look at the poor little girl."

Embarrassed, I stared at the two or three hairs that were left on my daughter's scalp. Then came her excuses.

"But Mom, I was so hot!"

Saturday at lunch time Mona was irritable. She was withdrawn and ignored my pleas to try to get her to eat. Her father finally got fed up and decided to try exercising a little authority.

"Mona, that's enough, now eat something," he said sharply.

She was crying, softly and sadly. The sounds of her sobs broke my heart, but I restrained myself, thinking that André was doing it for her own good. But it seemed to me as if something really was wrong: Mona seemed to be having trouble breathing. Just a protective mother's imagination, I decided.

"Now stop your crying," André insisted.

Cut to the quick, Mona rose to go to her room to cry like a grown-up. She was making a strange sound every time she drew breath, a rattle that grew louder and louder. We stared at each other, frightened by the noise. We tried to calm her down, though we were anything but calm ourselves.

"What's the matter, Mona?"

"We didn't mean to bawl you out."

"Calm down now."

We were practically shouting, we were that anxious. The rattle grew harsher, and Mona became frightened by the sound coming from her own body. I had prepared myself for a moment like this. My hand was trembling, though I knew the number I had to dial by heart.

Finally the doctor in emergency answered. He could hear Mona's hoarse breathing which had begun to sound like barking as she grew more agitated. "It's probably false croup," he diagnosed.

I fought off my panic and silenced my pounding heart.

"She has leukemia (it hurt to say that word) and she's under-going treatment. Please, if you could tell her doctor . . ."

I asked for an ambulance. As a precaution, someone suggested oxygen. I had to stay calm and alert. I called a baby-sitter for Francis and looked for a blanket to wrap around Mona. André watched me spring into action; he considered doing a thousand different things and ended up doing nothing.

"Should I take the car?" he asked.

"I need you with me," I shot back. "Forget about the car."

"Who'll take us home?"

"Someone! Anyone! What does it matter?"

The few minutes that passed as we waited for the ambulance seemed like a lifetime. I wondered just what false croup was. I didn't want to get upset needlessly: that wouldn't help Mona. I managed to keep control of myself until the ambulance arrived.

"Did you bring the oxygen?"

"No."

I cursed the ambulance driver under my breath while he ran back to get it. Mona breathed more easily with the oxygen — and I caught my breath, too. The doctor's words came echoing back.

"Accept the fact that it's incurable and that she'll die. It will be less painful that way. If you don't, you'll bring yourself to the breaking point every time she has a relapse."

I knew that leukemia patients died because they could no longer fight infection. Mona shook me from my morbid thoughts. She was having trouble breathing again, and she kept pushing away the oxygen, twisting her neck as she gasped for air. We were only half-way to the hospital and traffic was at a stand-still. The driver put on the siren and we moved ahead. André and I jammed the imaginary accelerator pedal to the floor. But something was terribly wrong. Mona was still pushing away the oxygen.

"Maybe it's too dry in here. Turn off the heat." That was the problem. The ambulance windows steamed up and Mona began breathing more easily. She took oxygen from time to time while I prayed.

I'd never been in an ambulance before: this was my baptism. I was anxious to get out of this four-wheeled coffin. André was holding Mona tenderly in his arms. As he spotted the hospital up ahead, his shoulders slumped and his eyes closed as he breathed a sigh of relief.

The doctor sensed our panic and did his best to speak calmly and reassure us. "She'll get over it, there won't be any complications."

He told us that false croup seemed much more frightening than it really was, and his explanations were so convincing that we actually believed that Mona had begun to breathe more easily. With a wet towel under her nose, each breath she took was quieter than the one before. She was put into an oxygen tent filled with moisture and was attached to an I.V. bottle so that she could receive antibiotics every four hours without an additional injection.

I held her hand through the tiny opening in the tent. She had calmed down, and I was less afraid now, too, though my heart was filled with remorse. Why had I forced her to eat? Should I never be harsh with her again? Did I have to let her do whatever she wanted? Maybe it was the puppy; maybe she was allergic to it. I could hardly tell right from wrong any more. I began to drift, listening to my daughter's breathing, and, unconsciously, my breathing became deeper too.

Fear was gradually eating away at me. There were circles under my eyes, my stomach was tied up in knots, and my shoulders seemed permanently slouched. I realized that that was what would defeat me: fear. I'd be so afraid every time she had an attack that in the end I would give up and say, "Go ahead, take her, I can't fight any more." Then I would stop struggling and begin to prepare for my child's funeral.

The very thought was like the sting of a whip. I jumped up and gave myself a shake. Had I spoken those last words aloud? They seemed to be still echoing in my ears.

I went to André's side. His nose was pressed against a window, surrounded by the smell of disinfectant that he hated so much; he was gazing out at the autumn hills. He hadn't shaved and he was wearing his ragged weekend jeans. I looked as though I'd just gotten out of bed; we made quite a pair.

You could scarcely make out Mona in the tent. She was eating ice cream and seemed to have gotten used to her new lodgings. I felt relieved that she was in good hands; now it was time for us to go. She sensed that I was about to leave, and tried to put off the moment when she would be alone by asking for the bed pan. The tent was opened, and she clung to us, crying. Then she started making that barking sound again and the tent had to be closed to keep in the moisture. I blew her kisses, my heart breaking.

"Good night, honey, we'll be here first thing tomorrow morning."

And I left before I started crying too. André was pulling me by the arm. "Come on, we're better off leaving her now. Francis is downstairs with some friends. They've come to pick us up."

I knew that he was trying to remind me that Mona wasn't the only one who needed my attention. I had to trust the hospital staff to care for her when I wasn't there.

When the doctor advised me to get a little rest, I defended myself. "Do you think I'm being over-protective?"

"No. But she's not in any danger."

Those were the words I wanted to hear, and I believed them. For the first time in weeks, I would go to bed without my daughter sleeping across the hall. Her room faced ours and both doors were always open so that I would be able to hear the slightest sound she made. Every night I went to bed emotionally and physically exhausted, and I slept only because I had to. A part of me always remained awake, listening for my sick child. I concentrated all my love on Mona; the others could wait. It seemed as if my life as a woman and a wife was over. I could hardly imagine making love while my daughter lay sleeping a few steps away. But tonight I would sleep for myself alone and forget about the rest of them. I would make it up to them all later.

Francis had become difficult and ill-tempered. Every morning he would invent a new excuse for staying home with me.

"I've got a stomach ache."

I cajoled and encouraged him, but all he said was, "Mom, I'd like to cut off your head so I could put you in my book-bag. That way, when I was sad, I could take you out and kiss you." My heart went out to him.

His teacher had warned me, "His school work is fine, but at recess he often ends up in a corner by himself."

That Monday morning we had breakfast together, just the two of us, since André was still sleeping. Francis had me to himself for once. He had changed and I hadn't even noticed it. He had learned how to read. He wanted to show me, and I admired his skill, disappointed that I had missed that stage in his development. These last few weeks, he had been practising his reading with the baby-sitter.

"And you learned all that without my help."

"Do you think I read well?"

I ran my hand tenderly through his hair and said, "We'll take you out to eat at a real restaurant with grandpa and grandma. Would you like that?"

Of course he would. But I spoiled his happiness by announcing that the baby-sitter would be looking after him that afternoon.

"Your father and I are going out."

"Where are you going? I want to come, too!"

"No. We have to go out alone."

We left him in tears with some relatives. He couldn't understand why we didn't want him with us.

When we returned to the hospital, Mona was with her doctor. The medication seemed to have controlled her attack of false croup. The doctor was very pleased with her reaction to the drugs, and he told us he would take advantage of her hospitalization to give her her weekly injection and blood transfusion. He took the trouble to do all this on a Sunday, just to spare us another trip to the hospital and a day's wait.

He was standing there, looking very relaxed, one foot on a chair. "Why don't you take a break and go out and have some fun? Mona's doing fine, you can see that."

She looked at him trustingly, so we lingered only a few minutes more. We would go anywhere, it didn't matter. See the least stupid movie in town. The doctor was right — a little amusement wouldn't hurt.

We saw a war film, and the violent scenes tempered my enthusiasm for life a little. Soldiers were raping women; I let go of André's hand. The second film was a comedy, and by the time we returned to Mona's bedside, we were in good spirits.

The colour had returned to her cheeks. We knew someone else's blood was the cause, but we were happy with the results anyway. Mona was in a good mood. André clowned around and put my fur hat on sideways. Then he started in with her wig. It was wonderful to hear her laugh again, and that night we were almost happy. Later on we discussed the films; commented on what a good man the doctor was. And remembered Mona's excited laughter.

"Did you hear how happy she sounded? Just like before."

And I was happy too, pleased that André had taken me to the movies, even though I knew that it had been at the doctor's suggestion. I could just hear him saying, "You ought to take your wife out." But at least he was reaching out to me, and that evening there was a sort of peace between us. Tomorrow I would take up my role as nurse again. I had had two days off. The respite had not been long enough to give us a chance to reach some understanding, talk about the fears and sorrows that we no longer dared admit to one other. But at least we had managed to accept each other a bit more in our sadness.

Another person's blood provides only a few days of life; you need more than that to continue the fight. I wasn't feeling very well myself. My clothes had become too big, and there was a swelling in my throat that worried me. I showed it to Mona's doctor when I was there for a weekly visit. As if he could read my mind, he smiled and teased me, "It must be a nice fat cancer."

I hated that word. I tried to laugh it off but didn't succeed.

"Your sore throat is caused by stress," he said. "Have a glass of wine once in a while, maybe before meals. Try to relax and stop smoking so much. No more than ten cigarettes a day."

When Mona had first fallen ill, I had wanted to do something heroic to help cure her — like giving up cigarettes. But there seemed to be something too desperate about making such sacrifices. Now I would have to smoke less to keep myself in good health for Mona's sake.

As for the occasional drink, I used it to help untie the knots in my stomach. When I sat down to eat, after giving Mona her pills and cooking the meal, I would catch sight of my son's worried expression and my daughter's lifeless eyes and lose my appetite completely. So I would pour myself a glass of wine, and after the first two or three sips, I'd feel the warmth fill me.

"What are you doing?" André would say.

"Can't you tell? It helps me swallow and digest better. You want some?"

"No thanks. I've got to go back to school after dinner."

In the evening, the dishes done, when my throat was burning and hurting, I took the gin bottle, gargled a bit of the stuff for quick relief, then took a good pull to help me sleep. What else could I do to hang on?

In fact, that was all I was doing: just hanging on. Mona was looking paler, Francis was clinging to me more and more, and my husband was slipping away from me. He found his outlet in school activities. There were evenings when I waited for him to come through the door just to ask, "Do you think she's losing more colour? Does she need blood? I'm with her all day. I'm afraid I won't notice in time."

"That's all you think about."

I wheeled around and faced him. *That's all you think about!* Good God, what else should I think about?

Unable to say anything else, I shot back, "Look after the kids, I'm going out."

I walked out into the early winter evening and the cold hit me inside and out. I forced myself to walk to a friend's house where I collapsed into a chair and half listened to my friends comment on the latest news in town. In the middle of their chatter, whose sole purpose was to distract me, I interrupted, "I can't stand it any more! She's paler than ever. Now she's coughing too."

They listened to me patiently. "Maybe it's because you're with her all day."

And the man mentioned a young cousin in the States who had had a blood disease like Mona. "Guess what? She got married, just last year." Of course no one ever talked about the ones who died. Later, when I was comforted a little, they sent me home. I put the children to bed and cried out to God.

"Why are You doing this to me? What is it supposed to teach me?"

For the hundredth time, I thought of my pregnancy and Mona's birth. Had I taken some drug? I remembered her conception as if it was yesterday. We had planned her, and when she arrived, we were as happy as two human beings could be.

Of my two children, she was the sparkler, brimming over with life, always about to rush off on some new adventure. I used to call her my "Ray of Sunshine." I relived each of her childhood diseases, and I remembered how I had cared for her. Had I done everything the way I should have?

Ever since the beginning of Mona's illness, I had felt regrets. Because I had wanted to go back to work, wanted a little freedom, I had left the children with baby-sitters. I had wanted money, possessions — especially possessions — even if the children had to suffer a little. But now the quest for possessions was over; from now on, I would live only for what really mattered.

"Mona's coughing a lot," André announced. He didn't need to tell me.

After looking in on her, I thought about God again. Deep down, I wasn't blaming Him. God was goodness, and when I, too, was good, I felt close to Him. I often thanked Him for having given me life. And I resisted the temptation to get down on my knees and ask Heaven for favours.

One morning, after a particularly bad start, I decided to go and see a friend of mine and her children. My girl friend thought Mona looked particularly weak, and asked, "Is she going to go into remission?" And I badly wanted to believe that she would have a remission — at least one.

"Why don't you take her to see a healer?" she went on. "I'd try it if I were you."

I rebelled against the very idea. A healer! That was all I needed. Why not put your trust in medicine which has been searching for the answers for centuries? All the same, I took a closer look at how they worked, and I realized that what they were really selling were healing images that they projected onto an imaginary screen for their patients. Sometimes it worked; other times people would die from their beliefs. I didn't know why, but I wouldn't entrust my daughter to one of those people.

Instead I started to read up on Mona's disease. With a curiosity that bordered on masochism, I pored over the pages that described the evolution of the disease, and explained how children were often claimed by other infections because their resistance was so low. I never knew reading could hurt so much. That was my child they were talking about. But I wanted to understand. I wanted to be logical.

The reading material provided by the doctor talked about how to break the news to the parents: "It is the doctor's duty not to let the unfortunate parents nurture any false hope." He had certainly done his duty, this doctor of ours! So that was how he had learned his technique. Disappointed, I shut the photocopied pages and held my head in my hands. I wanted understanding, logic.

But who knew what to believe in? In medical science, that administered treatments to prolong the patient's life, knowing that the patient would die anyway? In the God of my childhood, who held life and death in His hands? Or in the healers, who offered dreams of recovery?

Later that day, André came home, returning from the outside world, where life carried on.

"Hey, guess what? I met some interesting people. They live in Three Rivers. They're like us — you know, a Quebec woman who married an American guy. He hardly speaks French at all."

I half-listened to him. I had other things on my mind. Then I heard him say, "I'd like to invite them over for supper Saturday night. What do you think?"

I got my back up right away. "What are we going to tell them when they see Mona?"

I could picture it now; introducing the family. All those questions to answer. Why is she so swollen? What happened to her hair? Why isn't she playing? Why is she so pale?

But André had already figured it out. "We'll eat later, like around eight o'clock. We'll have a few drinks before dinner. By that time the kids will be asleep."

I bit my lip. I thought he was being unreasonable. As if I didn't have enough to do already. But I couldn't find any good arguments against the idea and he was expecting an answer.

"All right." Still a bit unsure, I added, "Wait a minute. What's *she* like?"

"She's real nice," he said, smiling. "She teaches English. Pretty, blonde — "

"I'll bet!"

I got ready for the dinner, even though I thought it was hardly appropriate, inviting people to dinner and having a good time. Yet in spite of everything I wanted it to be a success. But Mona wouldn't leave my side for a minute.

"Mom, I want to go skating."

I knew very well that it was just one of her whims. She would end up tired and whimpering and I'd have to carry her home.

"I don't have time," I told her. But I caught myself right away. Live for what's important. Sure, but everything's important . . . everything but the housework. I tossed my rag into the corner.

"All right, we'll go skating. But not for long. And I don't want you to start crying when I tell you it's time to go home."

Mona was surprised to discover that she wasn't ruling the roost today. Her mother was busy thinking about these strangers who were coming for dinner. Sitting at his desk, André was working on next week's courses. He wasn't worried about a thing; he left it all to me. He got up to look for a note that he'd left in our bedroom, and as he passed, he suddenly took me in his arms.

"I love you, you know," he said.

I didn't know what to think. He said he loved me. Was that what loving was all about? I looked into his eyes, searching for some truth to hold on to. I felt my heart swelling. I was afraid I'd start crying.

"You know that, don't you? I love you."

"I don't know anything any more."

Then I went out with Mona. She was waiting for me by the door, bundled up in her coat, a red wool cap on her head. She looked normal . . .almost.

"That hat looks good on you, Mo."

As if Mona understood what was expected of her, she only woke up once during dinner to go to the bathroom.

"She has leukemia," André explained briefly. "She's undergoing treatment, and the medication has made her lose her hair."

He said it as naturally as if he were talking about a toothache. And that was that. He continued his dissertation about the right way to teach English as a second language in Quebec.

At first our guests were speechless: the word "leukemia" had caught them off guard. But André passed over the subject so lightly that they continued chatting away as if nothing was the matter.

I stopped listening. I didn't know whether to admire or hate him for being able to dismiss our daughter's illness so easily. I wondered what would have happened if we had discussed her condition with a great helping of tragic detail. I could see the faces growing sad, the hearts beating faster, the men holding back their tears.

I passed our guests the salad and thought, he didn't really lie. He simply told the truth and dropped the less pleasant details that would have kept him from enjoying himself this evening.

I considered his confident smile as he poured the wine. The other woman was pretty and seemed interested by what he was saying, but it was obvious that she was totally in love with her Dick, so I laid my worries to rest.

After I had finished putting away the dishes and wiping the ashtrays, we went to bed. André gazed at me tenderly, but he didn't push it. As usual I was exhausted and felt a little lost. I was always worried about tomorrow, always on the alert, ready to act in case of emergency, ready to go to the hospital again. It was almost as if I was expecting something to happen.

Mona tried to attract my attention as she called out as loudly as she could, "Mommy, phone for you!"

"You shouldn't answer the phone, dear. People can't hear you with your voice."

My mother was on the line. She forgot all about what she had to say and demanded, "What's the matter with her now? Has she lost her voice?"

Yes, she had. A tiny broken voice was such a pitiful, sickly thing. What could I do, Mona was losing everything — her hair, her voice, her beauty, her shape.

"She developed a little ulcer on her vocal cords," I explained.

My mother had called to tell me about the novena to Saint Joseph that she had begun. But she had been so distracted by the sound of Mona's faint voice that for a moment she forgot what she was calling for. Eventually, however, she remembered her mission and she continued, "I'll come on Saturday. I have a medal for Mona."

I didn't show much enthusiasm and she didn't force the issue. "Did you get the book I sent?" she asked. To inspire me, she had mailed me *Miracles of Your Mind* by Joseph Murphy. The book was brimming with positive thoughts and anecdotes.

"I got it. It doesn't stop me from being unhappy, but when I think about what's in the book, it takes my mind off my troubles."

That was enough to encourage my mother. At least she's reading it, she must have thought to herself. So she went on. "I pray for Mona every night. I want you to know that. I picture her like she was before, when she was all right. I imagine her just glowing with health."

She was doing all the talking and when she realized it, she cut her monologue short. "You should try, too. I know it's hard for you. You're with her every day and all you see is her sickness."

I hung up, wondering if my mother had all her wits about her. What was she really trying to tell me? Picture her glowing with health. Picture her cured. But how in the world could I picture that?

The next day I had to take Mona to Emergency for a shot of antibiotics. In the same room was a little retarded girl who must have been around six years old. Her eyes were like a fish's eyes protruding from her head, with no colour or life. Her body was puffy and shapeless, with short little limbs and narrow fingers. Her mother looked at her lovingly and called her "my little treasure."

I thought to myself that the poor lady couldn't see straight. And it was a wonderful thing that she couldn't.

The doctors crowded around the retarded girl. She didn't have much idea of what was expected of her and her mother explained things to her carefully and lovingly with strange sounds that must have been their secret language. Then the girl finally opened her mouth and took the thermometer between her slack lips.

I watched them struggle to keep the girl alive. Somebody believed in that being's existence. I turned to Mona: at least her eyes sparkled with intelligence, and I thanked my lucky stars for that. I, too, would go on fighting. I had no idea what weapons I would use, but I would try them all if I had to.

Later, as I was doing the wash, I read *Miracles of Your Mind*. "If you want something but expect the opposite, you'll never get what you want." I was beginning to see what the author was getting at, as I thought of all those times in my life when I had wanted something and, more often than not, had gotten it because I imagined myself coming out on top.

I looked up from the book. Mona had just taken her cortisone. She was sitting down with her finger over a lighted lamp. I was hoping that the heat from the bulb would break the abcess that had started to form. With Mona, the slightest scratch was an invitation to infection.

"It hurts so much, Mommy," she whimpered. "You don't know how much."

"Keep your finger by the lamp, honey. The doctor said it would bring it to a head faster." Since I figured that I was responsible for Mona's infections, I added Javex to the wash to sterilize anything she might come in contact with. Physically I was doing everything I could think of, but I knew that deep in my heart I was still dragging my feet.

Seeing how much attention his sister was getting, Francis decided to claim his share. He wanted to know if we loved him as much as Mona and he came down with pneumonia. His fever climbed to 104°. This time when I called the doctor — and I called him nearly every day — I said, "It's not Mona this time. My son is very sick. He's not eating, he has a high fever and I'm worried. I can't get to the hospital."

For once the doctor came just for Francis, who suddenly seemed to be on the road to recovery. Everyone showered attention on him, even Mona. When she was in a good mood, she took him his juice.

Incredible, the way all these things had happened within two months. I was willing to believe that someone had cast a spell on me. I scurried from bed to bed. The children controlled everything. I cooked meals they didn't even touch and no sooner had I put everything away than one of them asked for something else.

The doctor stressed that Francis had to have plenty of fluids. "Give him anything you can. He has to increase his intake of liquids."

Francis and Mona were the masters of the house. If one of them wanted a kiss, I had to run over to the other to prevent jealousy. If I told one a story, the next minute I had to start with the other's favourite tale. Francis complained a lot more than Mona. He complained about his stomach ache, nausea, his headache, and more than once he sobbed that he'd rather be dead. I begged him not to say those words.

"You're a big boy, you should have your own little goals in life, too."

I was so tired. Francis hadn't eaten a thing for four days and his fever shot back up. The doctor came and gave Mona antibiotics to protect her as much as possible from the treacherous virus.

"Good luck," he said as he left.

"I tried to disinfect things as much as I could."

He shrugged his shoulders. "That doesn't make much difference."

Something inside me urged me to struggle on. I disinfected the whole house. I had spray germicides, I put Javex into everything I washed, I even stuck camphor under the children's pillows. I'd do anything to save them.

Meanwhile, we had forgotten all about the dog, and one night he started to cough and tried to vomit. I was furious. Was it his turn now? I'd reached my limit. He could drop dead as far as I was concerned; I had my hands full with the kids. But Mona cried and wanted us to take care of the puppy.

"We don't have enough money to take him to the vet's."

"Take some money from my bank, Mommy."

"Take mine, too," Francis begged.

Like a thief, I broke open their piggy banks. I managed to scrape together ten dollars and summoned the baby-sitter. Kiki was wrapped up in a blanket.

Diagnosis? Pneumonia and bronchitis. The next day, the dog took his antibiotics along with the children! What a farce! I felt as if some malevolent spirit was pulling the strings. Who was sending me all this misfortune? Or was I attracting it?

My mother arrived for a quick visit. She had brought a Saint Joseph medal for Mona. Nervously, she said that she knew a boy whose leukemia had been cured by the saint. In hushed tones, she tried to convince me to give her free rein.

"It certainly can't do any harm," she insisted. "We have to reach the child's subconscious with something concrete. Let me try."

I was uneasy. "I don't want to make her dependent on anything, especially relics."

"I just want to talk to her. The medal is only to help her understand."

I decided to close my eyes and let her perform her little rite. After all, why not? What harm could a little medal and an invocation do?

My mother went into the children's room where Mona was lying in the dark, half-asleep. She told Mona a story about a hero who was cured because he was convinced he would get better. Only my mother's believing eyes and the medal shone in the dark. Mona watched her attentively. The medal had come right from the oratory, just for her, my mother said. She put the medal on Mona's stomach. Mona wanted so much to believe.

"Good Saint Joseph, make Mona better."

Mona was very impressed. She promised to repeat the ceremony every night, placing the medal on her stomach and pronouncing the invocation. Soon she fell asleep, full of trust, with Saint Joseph under her pillow, next to the camphor which, they said, had the power to kill germs.

My mother didn't stay long. She found an excuse to leave, but I knew that the sight of Mona, becoming less and less recognizable, was causing her too much pain. She found my house suffocating with its disease and her poor daughter struggling in the midst of it. Her son-in-law was at his office and she didn't know what to think of him any more. He seemed to have been struck dumb by everything that had happened. Was he paralyzed? Couldn't he see what was happening? Unable to help, she escaped after entrusting our souls to God.

Francis insisted on having his own medal. A little later, an exact duplicate arrived in the mail.

When I saw how pleased the children were with their medals, I prayed along with them. I used to do that before Mona got sick. They would invent a prayer themselves in which they thanked heaven for all the good things and asked the guardian angel to stay by our side and protect us. I always liked the idea of a fine, handsome angel helping us choose between good and evil. Who could claim that none existed?

Mona wanted to have the medal on her stomach. I hesitated.

"Grandma told me to."

"Tell me what Grandma said."

Her story was so full of innocent faith that I couldn't resist. "You have to really concentrate on what you're saying."

"Good Saint Joseph, help Mona get well."

My younger brother called me.

"Where are you?"

"In Sherbrooke on business."

"Why don't you come over? You're only a few miles away."

But he said he was too busy. I ignored his excuses; I knew that he preferred to look the other way, too. I decided to give him a complete rundown whether he liked it or not.

When he asked "How are things?" I told him, "Haven't you heard? Mona lost her voice again. All she can do is whisper. You can't imagine how tiresome that is. I have to concentrate just to pick up what she's trying to say. She gets mad if I don't jump when she says jump." Why was I saying all this? I didn't have anything against him.

"You've got to hold on."

That was exactly what I used to tell myself, in the old days, when I was overflowing with confidence. I wanted him to say more, so I went on, "Francis is sick, too. To top if off, he spends all day telling me how he wishes he was dead."

"For Christ's sake, stop it!"

I almost smiled. It was funny to hear him swear instead of saying all the encouraging words he had intended. He was so young and earnest. Before he hung up he told me again, tersely, not to give up.

No sooner had I put down the receiver than Francis began wailing again.

"Mom, it hurts all over. I want to die."

I grabbed him by both arms. "If you don't stop saying that, I don't know what I'm going to do with you. I'm tired of hearing you talk like that, understand? Fed up!"

Seeing how taken aback he was, I carried on. "Take off your clothes and get into bed like the doctor told you. That'll make your fever go down. You're not drinking enough either. I know, I know, it gives you an upset stomach, but at least try! Here, have some Seven-Up. You used to like it."

I was practically shaking him. He obeyed.

Everyone wanted to help. They were afraid, but they wanted to help anyway. One day an aunt of mine phoned to express her sympathy. She had gone through more or less the same thing; last year, her husband had died of cancer. I had heard of the dignity she maintained until the end. A devoted wife, she had cared for her husband as best she could, and above all, she had remained calm. My dear aunt spoke of the serenity with which one must face death. She never stopped telling me how she sympathized with my situation, a poor defenceless woman stuck with a dying child.

In a resigned voice, she urged me to give in. "Just accept it, don't try to fight it. It's the best way, believe me. It hurts less that way, you'll see."

You'll see, you'll see . . . She knew what she was talking about. She had seen it all. Elbows on my knees, my head in my hands, I slumped down on the carpet between two chairs and cried. Were all my struggles a mistake?

The children were watching me. How long had they been there?

"Why are you crying, Mommy?"

I couldn't tell them that a voice on the phone had told me to accept the death of one of them. You don't say things like that to children. You set their dreams racing with beautiful tales, otherwise they will never want to grow up. I held them both in my arms and promised not to cry any more.

"Mom's very tired. Come on, why don't you help me pick up your toys?"

Then my sadness changed to anger. All somebody had to do was call up and say any old thing and I changed right into the person they expected me to be at a time like this: sad and discouraged. I had lost all sense of direction. Why go back and forth, up and down like a cork on the waves, chased from pillar to post by other people's attitudes? What was *my* goal, *my* dream? I felt the colour returning to my face, I felt alive again.

I put the kids in front of the TV and stopped their usual quarrel. "No fighting about the program."

Without the slightest feeling of guilt, I let Francis watch what he wanted to.

"Tomorrow I'll decide who gets to watch what."

I sat in my favourite chair watching the children in front of the television. I felt terribly divided. I was losing my strength somewhere between hope and despair. By now I had learned to live twenty-four hours at a time, but I had stopped dreaming, stopped imagining what beautiful things the future might hold. I never let myself think of the future, never let myself hope. I was too afraid that my imagination would lead me to the cemetery.

The shadow of death was poisoning my way of living, of loving my children and my husband. I had learned to reject images of sadness, but I had nothing to replace them with. How could I find an antidote without becoming irrational?

You'd have to be crazy to think that a medal could cure you. You'd have to be crazy to think that tomorrow would be brighter when you knew that you were getting old and that death was waiting for you at the end of your journey. You'd have to be crazy to think that life was beautiful when it was nothing but a struggle between good and evil, sickness and health, hatred and love.

Of course it was irrational to believe in love, when one out of every two marriages ended in divorce or separation. Yet despite the statistics, my heart still believed in success, not failure. I had believed in love, even when everything seemed lost. In love, in life — you have to believe in it, even if it makes no sense. Suddenly everything came clear. My dream — it had almost disappeared. I had almost let the course of events wipe it away.

I wondered how I could believe in it again.

"Healers sell images of healing."

"Don't expect anything if you're convinced you won't get it."

"Picture her in good health, picture her the way she used to be."

"Medals help you get better."

"The Lord giveth, the Lord taketh away." But why do I have a God?

Put your mind on something else, my husband said.

The doctor fulfils his role by treating your child even though he knows the case is hopeless. But what was my role?

The sun had almost set in my heart, yet I still wanted my child to live.

But did I really want it or didn't I?

I thought about my dream all day. I wanted to redefine it. What had kept me going this long? What was my goal and where was I headed?

I remembered all the good things that had happened in my life, and the afternoon went by more quickly than usual. The children were in a bad mood and I catered to them with a sly half-smile.

When André came home, I greeted him with a glint in my eyes. We went to bed; he turned toward the wall, as he had felt obliged to for so many weeks. I looked at him anxiously and was frightened by what I saw. We had let so much go by! Tonight I realized how much damage my dream had suffered. What had happened to love?

I looked for some kind of opening. I had no idea how he would react after my long silence. If only Mona would stop coughing, it might be easier to break the ice. What I had to say couldn't wait any longer. I got up and gave her some honey for her throat. I closed our bedroom door almost all the way. André realized something was afoot and he watched me out of the corner of his eye.

I made the first move. "Look . . . look at what it's doing to us," I whispered. And he was in my arms before I even finished the sentence. Or did I end up in his? It didn't matter. I had stopped

86

bearing a grudge against him for not understanding me. I didn't even understand myself. I should never have made those demands of him. I should have just been satisfied with being there. With him. Together. I hated the woman I had become. A martyr who was great at taking the blows but who avoided committing herself to anything definite.

"I'm sorry for everything. I didn't even know what I was saying." I kissed him.

I had been holding on for the sake of the children, but my maternal instinct had destroyed the very thing that had made me a mother in the first place.

I had wanted to build, live a thousand lives. But I had stopped building, too busy warding off life's blows. That wasn't living.

His tortured face was on my breast. How could I have believed that I was the only one to suffer? He too loved and suffered. I clung to him, I glimpsed his dream and mine, and I wanted them to come true. We had wanted to be individuals, married but free. But by saying yes to love I knew now that I was accepting both joys and sorrows — even heavy sorrows like these.

When I felt him come into me, I exploded. All the tension of the last weeks poured out my throat. I sobbed, I cried. I felt bound to a greater strength, to a source of life.

André brought me gently back to earth.

"Not so loud, love, you'll wake up the kids."

We made love so well that the memories of my pleasure were wonderfully misty.

Nestled in his arms, I talked things over with myself. I had to change — change inside. I knew that my strength lay within me. By living twenty-four hours at a time, I had let myself be shaped by the word temporary, expecting each day to bring me closer to the end. I had been submitting myself to life. From now on, I would take life by the horns.

André was sleeping. I moved his arm higher up, around my neck, so I'd be more comfortable and able to think. For starters, I would act differently with Mona. You don't treat a dying child the same way as a child who has some passing childhood disease.

You give a dying child a toy with tears in your eyes, because you think it might be his last. You forgive him anything. You put yourself in debt to satisfy his slightest whim, you become his slave. You never discipline him. Why bother? You can't hold anything back from a child who will never grow up. You give him everything: your time, your love, your health and attention. Everything. And the child becomes aware of his power. With a doomed child, you live as if he were about to die. You love him with a stifling, killing love.

But on the other hand, when you had a child with a bad cold, you cared for him as best you could, but in a different way. You spoiled him a little to sweeten the days that he had to spend indoors instead of going out to play with his friends. But that was nothing like the funereal attitude that you unconsciously adopted toward a dying child.

From now on, out of love, I would believe in the impossible, I would believe that my daughter would live. I'd treat her as if she was going to get better. I'd live an irrational dream. My hands would be gentle when I bathed her, but they would no longer be sad. My kisses would be filled with love, but never again would they have the bitter taste of final farewells. My eyes would be vigilant and watch for the time when special care was needed, but never would they watch for death. From now on, we would await life in this house. We would wait for good news.

At the same time I would have to find a way to protect my dream. No use mentioning it to the doctors, they would only demolish it in a flood of logic — statistics and blood-count reports. This would be a secret Mona and I would share.

I was sure Mona would be happier this way. Who could be happy being treated like someone on death row? Francis would stop being so concerned; there would be no more competition with his sister who had her illness as a sure-fire attention-getting device. Besides, when a woman knows that her child is going to get better, she can put him aside a little and think of her husband. She can make love again. She can think of her own needs, her own dreams.

Part III

Mona's treatments were nearly over and the blood tests showed almost no change, except that the platelet count was slightly higher. Her overall condition would have made a hangman weep. Her body refused to fight infections. She had become hard to deal with because of all the treatments and medication. She would throw a tantrum for no reason, but would rarely cry when she was actually in pain.

Mona had spent the last fifteen minutes sitting on the toilet, with André keeping an eye on her. She was bent over double, a stubborn look on her face. He waited patiently as she tried to pee.

"Why don't you go out and play? You can try later."

Her eyes intent and the muscles in her neck straining, she screamed, "No, I've got to go!"

Frustrated, André came back to the kitchen with Mona crying in the background. "My bottom hurts!" Stubbornly, she remained perched on the toilet, just in case. She didn't want to wet her pants. Finally André grabbed her and she threw another fit. He managed to calm her down by showing her the big red circle that the seat had engraved on her bottom. I tried to think of some way of solving the problem by cutting down the time she spent on the toilet. A big pan might do the trick. Mona's backside touched the bottom of it, and that kept her from always rubbing the same spot. The big yellow pan followed her wherever she went in the house; she always felt as if she had to go but never managed to urinate more that a few drops at a time. We put the pan on a chair and played Snakes and Ladders as we waited for her to go. For a while, we even forgot about the damned pot.

"Go ahead, Mo, it's your turn. You're almost at the end of the board."

Mona threw the dice, concentrating hard on getting a high number. She won! Everybody shouted, and in the general uproar, she managed to urinate a little.

"It burns, Mommy."

Mona's personality was changing. It was as if she wanted to make someone pay for her suffering. She became meticulous, always afraid of smelling of urine, and washing her backside became a regular ritual. She insisted that her every wish be granted, right down to the most insignificant details. If not, she launched into inconsolable wailing.

At the hospital, I was reassured as usual that it was all due to the drugs. Kidney stones had started to form. I was beginning to suspect that she might be taking too much medication, but I didn't think it right to question the doctors' judgement. After all, they were working for my child's well-being, and I wanted to trust them. They asked me to measure all the liquids that Mona drank and excreted, and to inform them immediately if what came out was lower than a certain level. I measured everything carefully. I wanted to catch the danger in time, but without being in a constant state of panic. I had to learn to live with that contradiction too.

I knew that some children with leukemia were undergoing the same treatment as Mona, but they were isolated in sterilized rooms, with no visitors allowed. Isolation was maintained for the duration of the treatment, eight to ten weeks. Mona, on the other hand, underwent treatment at home, surrounded by germs, with her mother as nurse. All the responsibility rested on my shoulders and I sometimes wondered if I could handle it. As a matter of course, I reported all changes to the doctor. We managed over the phone, with a visit from time to time when it was needed; that way, Mona was spared the hospital. The pharmacist was always ready to help.

By now I was acquainted with all the specialists who worked

under the head pediatrician. I knew who had the most influence and who had the last word when it came to a decision. I found out that they had consulted a doctor from Montreal. When they didn't agree among themselves, I could feel it. I wanted them to think I was strong so they would tell me everything. The more I knew, the better I could help and understand.

Mona was crying, bent over in pain. Her stomach hurt. I reached the doctor who, half-asleep, told me, "Give her a 222." It was as if he was saying, Knock her out, it'll stop the pain and then we can both get back to sleep.

I thanked him all the same. "If you weren't there I don't know what I'd do. Thanks again."

I cut the pill in half. Mona was absorbing enough medication as it was. If I couldn't put her to sleep with a half dose, I'd think of something else.

Mona slept for two hours, and I picked up a few moments of sleep as well. Whenever I could these days, I collapsed into a chair. It was the only way to hang on. Patiently, André put up with the schedule that Mona forced on us. Anything was better than seeing his daughter in a hospital.

She woke up in the middle of the night.

"Mommy, come here. There's blood in my pee."

I jumped up. Everybody in the house knew you had to watch for blood in urine or the stool. The toilet was never flushed until I had a look. Mona pointed at the bottom of the little pot that was used for measuring her urine. I bent over and spotted a little stone as sharp as a needle. There were a few beads of blood on it.

Weary but relieved, Mona announced, "My tummy doesn't hurt any more."

"It's all over, it won't hurt any more. This little stone was what was hurting you. Now go back to sleep, sweetheart."

Mona had a trusting nature. Her thin white legs propelled her into bed. Her head, with its few tenacious hairs, lay on the pillow. And underneath it, she felt for the miraculous medal.

I wanted to call the doctor. Blood in the urine was serious. I was always afraid of not reporting some important symptom soon enough. But André convinced me to wait until morning.

"Don't disturb him. There's no reason to. She's sleeping peacefully."

When I did phone the news to him in the morning, he said in a satisfied voice, "At least her pain will be reduced." He didn't sound very enthusiastic, but at least Mona's pain was gone for the time being, and I took advantage of the reprieve to invite her friends over. I asked their parents not to say anything, and I thanked them in advance for their discretion, as if that meant they would do as I had asked.

The children arrived, bringing gifts that Mona hardly looked at. Their happy, boisterous manner quickly wore her out. I sent them home, explaining, "She can't play for too long because she's sick. But she'll be better soon, and then you can stay all afternoon."

Slowly but surely, Francis was getting back to normal. He had had two courses of antibiotics to rid him of his pneumonia. He was still thin, but he would eat a little as long as he could choose what he ate and when he ate it. To encourage him, I asked our visitors to forget about Mona for a while and spend more time with Francis.

"I think Mona's getting tired of all this attention. She feels like she's under a microscope, and it's getting on her nerves."

How could I ask them to ignore a child who had gone bald and become deformed by cortisone? But there was something insulting about the way everyone made such a fuss over her. I wanted to say, if you love her too much, it means you really don't love her enough. But would anyone know what I meant?

By the time her treatment was over, Mona was at the mercy of every germ. Her cough returned, the ulcer reappeared on her vocal chords and cut her voice to a whisper again. In the medicine chest there were potions for absolutely everything. Decongestants, throat-soothers, cough suppressants for when her nagging cough kept the whole house awake.

I asked the doctor whether it would be better to keep Mona inside, so she wouldn't catch a cold or fall prey to some new germ. He told me it made no difference. And once again I wondered whether he was letting her go out just to grant her a final wish.

Nevertheless, one day when Mona was down in the dumps, I said in a cheerful voice, "Come on, let's go skating." Two blocks away was a little rink. We started out, remembering to bring a little pot of honey to soothe her coughing fits.

I had scraped together enough money to buy snowsuits for the children. There would be time enough later to worry about finances. For the time being, Mona was warm and cozy and that was all that mattered. Like all the other mothers, I tried to teach her how to skate.

"Go on, try it by yourself now." And I would catch her before she fell.

Back at home, Mona began to cough harder.

"Have a spoonful of cough syrup. It'll take the tickle out of your throat."

Mona realized I was treating her as if it really were just a tickle in her throat. She could sense how I'd changed lately. I was no longer so worried if the children scarcely touched their food at mealtimes.

"You'll eat when you're hungry," I would say casually, and I would make up for their meagre appetites by giving them cheese and fruit for snacks. There were plenty of other, more important things to insist on.

When he came home from school, André kissed us both. "How are my girls?"

Mona liked him to treat her and me as equals. And we told him about the little activities we had managed to do that day, although coughing fits kept interrupting the story. André and I exchanged pained glances.

"Maybe I shouldn't have let her go out this afternoon," I said. "I'll put her to bed soon and give her some syrup to help her sleep."

But tonight the syrup had no effect. Mona was coughing constantly. Not knowing what else to do, close to panic, I called the doctor again — for the hundredth time.

"Doctor, Mona is coughing so much, I don't know what to do. I gave her that syrup that usually puts her to sleep. It made her drowsy, but she's tossing and turning, and she hasn't stopped coughing."

He listened and breathed a sigh. Why was he sighing like that? He must have been tired too. My heart was pounding. I wished I hadn't disturbed him. From the background came the sound of Mona's hacking cough.

"Listen, there's something you should realize . . ."

I hated it when he talked like that. It made me hold my breath.

"It hurts you more than it hurts her. Mona has no idea she's going to die."

I must have got him at a bad time. He couldn't have wanted to say that. I hung up in worse shape than before. He had never been so brutally frank. "It hurts you more than it hurts her." What else had he said afterwards? Something about a tap to see how her marrow was responding to treatment.

I thought of the medication and what it did. Like a catchphrase learned by heart, I repeated my lesson. Destroy the leukemia cells starting with the marrow. They couldn't save the healthy cells, but the child would grow new cells, supposedly healthy cells, and not die before they did their job. Maybe she couldn't tolerate these strong drugs any more. A marrow biopsy was a good idea: at least we'd know where we stood . . .

André watched me struggling with the possibilities, and he could guess what sort of conversation I had had with the doctor. In a broken voice, I said, "The Doctor . . ." but got no further. I managed to get up and go to his side.

"You can imagine what he told me."

My voice was steady. He was about to speak but I cut him off. "Don't talk. Kiss me."

He kissed me tenderly and stroked my hair.

"I'll be all right. I need to get some sleep. She has to have a bone marrow tomorrow."

Then suddenly I said, "I hate these biopsies. If you can take time off without losing pay, why don't you come with me?"

Bitterly, I criticized him for not lying to the principal of his school.

"Tell him you're sick. The unions are stupid. They want days off for funerals. What good does it do to visit people after they're dead? But they don't let you take time off to be with your loved ones."

To stop myself from crying again I got up and put the humidifier next to Mona, aiming the steam at her face. I leaned over to look at her puffy eyes; her face had become wider than it was long. The unrecognizable face of a child born of love. I tried with all my might to picture her as she was before. I could almost see her, with her pretty curly hair and healthy rosy cheeks. In my memory, she skipped and jumped. "My Ray of Sunshine . . ." She was always dashing off somewhere. I smiled when I thought of how many times I had cautioned her to slow down. "You're like a cyclone when you go by." If there was one person on this earth who could get out of a fix like this, it was Mona. I believed it the way I believed the sun would rise tomorrow.

I whispered in her ear, "Sleep well, my love. You'll see, you'll get better. Do you hear me? You'll get better!"

I went back to bed, and the doctor's words haunted me. *What if he was wrong?* What if the massive doses of drugs were keeping Mona from rebuilding her blood? But there was no way of knowing, and no use getting grey hairs now. For the sake of my family, for Mona and for myself, I had to get some sleep.

The examining table was set up in the middle of the out-patient clinic so that the two doctors and the nurse could circulate more freely. They were waiting for the technician and his sterilized marrow biopsy kit. When Mona recognized the place she got panicky and wanted to turn around. She knew what was going to happen; she remembered only too well. Two months earlier she had gone through the same thing. How different she had been back then! She had been a pretty little girl with a sweet smile. She could be charming with the doctors and nurses. But this time she stared at them like a frightened animal. Her face was closed, her lips tight.

They hurried to administer the anesthetic before she threw a tantrum. Through her half-sleep, I heard her cry, "Mommy! Mommy!"

I left the room: there was nothing left for me to do there. I paced the corridor like a caged animal. The sound of her pitiful cry echoed in my ears. I turned on my heels and looked through a slit in the door. The doctors were still waiting for the technician. Mona was out but the anesthetic didn't last long. The doctor took the opportunity to give her her Vincristine for the week. Another dose? I didn't like what was happening. The doctor was irritated at having to wait. Would they tell me the same thing as the first time? That her marrow was completely shot? I paced the hallway to calm my nerves, crying softly.

A pediatrician who was following Mona's case spotted me.

"What's the matter?"

"Mona's in that room. I'm so worried."

"Oh!" he breathed, obviously relieved. "You scared me. I though you had heard some bad news."

He was very busy, but took the time to chat for a minute.

"We have to examine the bone marrow because at the beginning of the disease, we don't really know how to administer the medication, what quantity to give. That's why we have to analyze her marrow."

And, sensing that he had pacified me, he continued on his way.

When he talked about the beginning of the disease, I was afraid it was the end. White cells fought infection; could too many drugs kill her? I leafed through a magazine, but nothing interested me. I jumped every time a door opened. I wiped my sweaty palms on my skirt.

"It's over," I heard someone say.

The technician went off with the samples to analyze. Mona was lying there, exhausted, her lifeless eyes half closed. I dressed her. She was as limp as a rag doll and twice as hard to handle. It was five o'clock already and everyone had left the hospital. Outside it was snowing and people were leaving to avoid being caught by the early December storm.

I felt too exhausted and alone to drive, so I called all over town to find somebody who would drive us home. One of my friends had gone shopping, the other wasn't home. The telephone rang in the emptiness of deserted houses. I was irritated — if only André were here! But I didn't bother calling him. By the time he found a car and made it over. . . . It was too complicated.

Mona's snowsuit wouldn't go on properly and I had to be so careful. Her whimpering broke my heart; I couldn't stand seeing her suffer any more. Sweat was running down my arms. On top of it all, I had to put up with a nurse who wanted to chit-chat. Moved by pity, she took a stab at trying to help me. Who had sent her on this mercy mission anyway? What did she want from me?

"It's too bad, eh?" she said.

As if I had to be told! I restrained myself from giving her a piece of my mind. I knew it was too bad. I bit my lip; no use wasting energy on her.

"We'll be home in no time, Mona."

The doctor came in. "I hope you're a good driver."

"I'll be fine. I'll go slowly."

I was talking myself into being okay. He put his arm around my shoulders and gave me a squeeze, like an athlete getting a pep talk before a race. I lowered my eyes and blew off a lock of hair that had fallen in my eyes.

"My family is expecting me. I've got to go back and fix dinner. Thank you, Doctor."

Sitting in a wheelchair, Mona waited with the nurse for me to come back after I heated up the car. I sat her comfortably in the back seat and started out. The sky was very grey. It was snowing harder and harder. The roads were completely snowpacked. If we had an accident it would be all over! But I chose to be careful. I was hungry and groped in my purse for a cigarette. If I had the money, I'd buy some take-out food in a restaurant. One day, maybe. Driving carefully, I finally reached the house.

André came to meet me and carry Mona. "You look exhausted."

But I was too empty and too famished to answer. I got down to making supper. My stomach was grumbling. Mona described what they did to her. She had practically stopped coughing; at least the anesthetic had one good side effect. And it lasted all night. She didn't wake up once, which let me recuperate for the next day . . .

Mona was too weak to even move. She just lay on the couch now, day in and day out, watching us go about our lives. Only her ears were red, burning with fever. Every second breath, she burst out coughing. She had stopped speaking. She breathed and coughed, that was all, breathed and coughed.

I had to do something. I couldn't bear that look in my daughter's eyes, that defeated look.

"I think it's time to have her hospitalized," I finally said to André.

He hated cold hospitals, and he couldn't stand seeing her suffer any more. He opened his mouth and just like that, he said, "No. I'd rather . . . I want her to die at home."

"Don't you say that!"

I stopped myself from making a scene. Mona was watching us. She was my child too, and the decision was half mine.

André got ready to go to work. I didn't want him to go. I knew he was feeling badly too. "Leave me the keys to the car," I said, and when he had left I called a girlfriend. I didn't want to be alone at a time like this.

"I need you. Do you mind coming over?"

I didn't like to go against my husband's wishes, but I wasn't about to let my little girl die without lifting a finger. I got ready to go out, and from time to time I glanced out the window. If only it wasn't snowing so hard . . . If we had an accident, he'd be mad at me for not having listened to him. Nevertheless, I prepared myself to go out, and then I called the hospital. Mona's pediatrician was out, and I was relieved, in a strange sort of way. I was afraid he'd tell me there was nothing left to do. Suddenly I thought of the doctor who had talked about the beginning of

Mona's illness the day before. What was his name again? I had the feeling he could help me.

"Doctor . . . Doctor, I . . ."

"Yes?"

"Mona is in very bad shape. My husband . . . my husband wants her to . . . to end up at home. He wants her suffering to stop. (I was whispering so Mona couldn't tell how upset I was.) Please, do something. Can't you do something?"

He asked me for André's phone number, pulled him out of his classroom and talked to him for a good fifteen minutes. Meanwhile, Mona coughed and I waited.

I watched André walk up to the house, his head bent; he looked so sad. Without wasting a minute, he drove us to the hospital. I asked no questions. All that mattered was that he had agreed to have Mona hospitalized. Finally, he spoke.

"The doctor convinced me that she'd be better off in the hospital. They're equipped to handle these kinds of cases, I guess."

I wondered if "these kinds of cases" were the hopeless ones. I knew what André was thinking: this was the final journey to the hospital. Or maybe those were my own thoughts. I held my daughter stubbornly to my breast. The sky was white with snow.

"Mona, look how the sky changes when it snows. Can you see it, the way you're lying?"

She answered me with a cough.

"The doctor promised to get back to us as soon as he had the results of the biopsy from the lab," André said.

Finally we reached the hospital. I smiled at the nurse who, in my opinion, was the best one in pediatrics. She had a way of asking, "Aren't you feeling well, Mona?" that seemed to say, "You'll be better in no time."

Mona was suffering from double pneumonia and once again was put in a croupette. She didn't like being closed up, but she didn't have the strength to resist. She would be all alone in her room. A window looked out onto another room, where no visitors were allowed. The curtain wasn't completely drawn and we could see a twelve-year-old girl inside. She was watching TV as they gave her a transfusion, and she kept checking the needle stuck into her hand.

I turned away from that sad scene and reassured Mona. "You'll sleep better in the tent. I'll stay right here."

Do something, I can't stand hearing her cough, I wanted to shout. Finally the doctor appeared, dressed in sports clothes. He wasn't on duty. He was holding up a piece of paper in his hand. I examined his face to gauge what was written in the report.

"Very good," he said. "Have a look!" He handed me the piece of paper. My head was bursting with questions I couldn't put into words. What did good mean? I read it hurriedly. I wanted to take it in all at once. My eyes went immediately to a line written all in capital letters and underlined in red: NO BLAST CELLS. I must have read it wrong. That meant there were only healthy cells in her marrow! And those cells would make strong, healthy blood! I read the report again. I was frozen to the spot, afraid I'd explode. I stared at the doctor.

Holding back the shout in my voice, I stammered, "Her ... her marrow is in good shape. There aren't any malignant cells."

"That's what the report says."

It was if he had just announced that Mona was officially cured. I was so happy I covered Mona with kisses.

"See how good the results are?" I said, showing Mona the piece of paper.

Mona didn't understand what it was all about, but at least she stopped coughing for a few seconds. I didn't know what to do with myself, I certainly couldn't sit still. I had to tell somebody.

"I'll be right back, sweetheart, just a minute."

I ran to the pay phone and joyfully blurted out to my parents and friends that Mona was very sick, that she had to be hospitalized, she had double pneumonia, but her marrow was very good, even if she did have a bladder infection. They didn't quite follow me but why bother explaining? I was already dialing the next number.

The doctor doubled the cortisone dose to help Mona fight her pneumonia. She would become twice as swollen, but that didn't matter. He cut off all the anti-leukemia drugs. She had really had her fill; now her body had to be encouraged to regenerate new blood. Antibiotics, Tempra to lower the fever, ice-water baths. And I, Mona's mother, standing at the foot of her bed, I promised to give her all the love and lust for life that my heart contained.

Back at home that evening, I felt as if I had won a battle, though my sense of victory was tempered by a very real fear. I knew how serious her condition was; there was no room for illusions.

I wanted to be sure that Mona had everything she needed, as if she were still at home under my care, so I called the head nurse.

"How is she?"

They don't like giving bad news to parents, especially at eleven o'clock at night. At the other end of the line, the nurse stammered, "Well, her fever is pretty high. And her cough is pretty bad, too."

"Did you give her something? Is the doctor there? Did you call him?"

I was acting like a lioness pacing over her young. I had the feeling that they were being negligent. As I talked on the phone, I remembered how much trouble they had had installing the humidifier in the tent. Was this night nurse acquainted with Mona's case? I tried to explain everything to her at once.

"I tried to get a hold of the technician to repair the machine."

"Change the croupette, do something. I took her to the hospital so she'd be better off than at home."

Finally I took the edge off my voice and said, "Please, take care of her as if she were your own daughter."

The nurse promised she would.

"Thank you so much. I'll call back later."

I waited an endless hour, long enough for the medication to take effect. When I called back, Mona was sleeping and her fever had dropped below the danger line. The machine was working at full capacity, helping to clear her blocked lungs.

In the bottom of my heart I was convinced that my daughter was cured of leukemia, though I did my best to hide it because I knew it was insane. I wanted to do everything possible to cure her of that wasting pneumonia. For starters, I'd give myself a new look. As if this misfortune was only a passing thing, I took the rest of our money and went to the beauty shop. And when André paid me a compliment, my smile sparkled even more.

I stifled my pride and convinced a dress shop to give me credit on a suit that seemed made just for me. "No problem," the saleslady said. "We know each other well enough."

Of course we did! In this little town, everybody knew everybody else. I preferred to think that she didn't know about my situation. Anything to keep from spoiling the pleasure of being beautiful, of feeling on top of the world for once. I slipped on the new suit. It was of very good quality. André smiled and I forgot about the money owed for now.

Pleased with myself, I walked into Mona's room. Hands on my hips, I turned slowly like a model to show myself to best advantage.

"Do you like my hair, Mona?" I smiled.

What kind of question was that to ask a little girl without a hair left on her head? Enclosed in her croupette, Mona displayed total indifference. She was sulking because I had left her in there. I offered to play with her, but she refused to become interested in anything. Instead, she coughed. Unconsciously, I was starting to want to spit, as if to help her get rid of the stuff that was hampering her breathing. Once I realized what I was doing, I stopped that nervous reaction.

"You didn't eat anything, your tray is full. Do you want Mommy to bring you some treats from home?"

I started taking her her favourite foods from home. But she hardly took a bite of anything.

André took time off from work to be with Mona more often. Everybody liked her and wanted to help out. In the morning, her favourite nurse came to see her before starting work in the outpatient department. She would bring her children's books, but Mona gave her a downcast look and ignored her gifts. From inside her steamy croupette, she couldn't have cared less about the love people were showing her. She coughed instead.

The friends and family who went to spend some time with her in the evenings couldn't help but wince when they heard the nasty cough whose sound was both amplified and muffled by the oxygen tent.

"Poor child," some of them gasped. But I wasn't swayed by their pity, and I must have seemed heartless. I acted as though I hadn't heard a thing, chatting away as if Mona would be getting better soon. After all, why not? Her marrow was healthy. I ignored the pained expressions on their faces. All they saw was a child they could scarcely recognize, swollen, bald, with lifeless eyes and a sickly bad temper. But I was her mother and I saw something else. My view of the future was different from theirs now.

Tonight, dressed in my new outfit, with a little make-up on, I looked my best. André was at a conference, and we had arranged to meet in a restaurant at ten o'clock. I didn't know why I was so excited about this little foray into the outside world. I was going to meet some of his colleagues, and I told the whole story to Mona, as if it interested her. My voice was lively, but she didn't react. She sulked. I ignored her indifference and went on anyway.

"You know, Dad was elected president of the English Teachers' Association. That's very important to him."

I held her hand. It was lifeless except for the jerky movements of her hacking cough. Soon it would be time to leave. I decided to open the zipper that held in the steam and my daughter.

"Do you want to kiss me? I have to be going."

She burst into tears in my arms. She cried and moaned.

"What's the matter, Mona darling?" Then I answered for her. "You're fed up, aren't you? Fed up with all this medication and all these shots?"

She cried harder and harder, shaken by her cough. "I love you." I whispered. "You'll see, everything that's getting in the way of your breathing will go away. As soon as you're better, we'll take you home. I cross my heart, sweetheart."

The two days in the oxygen tent seemed like forever to her. She pressed up against me. Then she spat.

"See, it's coming out. Force it out, Mona, get it all out!"

When she finally calmed down, I asked one final favour of her. "Mo, try to smile. Just do that for me."

That was all I asked. Smile. Be bored and suffer — but smile anyway.

"And tomorrow, when Nicole comes to bring you some books, give her a nice smile. She misses your smile, you know. Are you going to try?"

I acted as if she had nodded yes. I wiped away the big tears that rolled down her shiny, swollen cheeks. Mona gently squeezed my hand. Yes, she would try.

Our goodbye ceremony usually lasted nearly an hour. But I didn't care. My intuition told me it was important for Mona to get out of herself and express what she felt.

But tonight André wanted to have his say.

"Kiss her goodbye and let's go, all right?" he said hurriedly. "She won't talk to us when we're here, but as soon as we're about to go, she starts hanging on."

Men just didn't understand. They thought that affection should be expressed during certain hours. As calmly as possible, I answered, "Don't ask so much of her all at once. Wait for me in the hall if it bothers you."

I took as much time as we needed. And when Mona had finally unburdened herself of everything she had been storing up in her little girl's heart, she and I agreed to call her father in. When he came in, she held back her tears to keep from disappointing him. He stroked her tenderly, spoke to her in a gentle voice and left, admitting that, though he liked women a lot, he didn't understand them.

Mona smiled. I closed the door triumphantly.

The next day Mona was willing to play inside her croupette. I slipped my hand into her little house and we played a card game. I did my best to lose and displayed great disappointment at the fact that she beat me so often.

"You're lucky, you know!" I told her more than once.

Mona ended up thinking she was on a sure-fire lucky streak. And when I decided to win one little game, just one, I couldn't even do it.

Glowing, Mona cried out, "See how lucky I am!"

I showed her the bright sun shining outside. I wanted so much to make my daughter feel life's strength, but in a language she would understand. So I talked about the puppy.

"He can't wait to see you again. He sniffs all around your bed, then he jumps on top and runs back to me."

Mona smiled, picturing Kiki's antics.

I talked to her about Christmas, too. I was making plans already. The house would be decorated in its holiday finery, but the real celebration would be in our hearts. In every way possible, I tried to make Mona want to return home.

Four more days went by before Mona was able to come out of her tent. As she was sitting on my lap, an intern who knew us well stopped by. Without thinking, he nodded his head in her direction and said, "These kinds of cases are always heartbreaking. There's just nothing we can do for these poor children." And he shook his head, a pained expression on his face.

The shock of it knocked me for a loop. I felt like a boxer who gets knocked out in the final second, just as he thinks he's about to win the title.

"But the latest tests showed that her marrow was in good shape!" I protested. "Didn't you see them?"

He hadn't. But he wasn't concerned about tests. All that mattered to him was the inevitable.

And I had been so caught up in making my daughter live that I'd forgotten all about it. But then, men created ways of counting off time and waved calendars in your face to remind you how fleeting life was — especially Mona's life. The intern went away, and I realized how fragile my impossible dream was. A little common sense broke it into a thousand pieces. I felt as though I was walking a tightrope. On one side were the harsh realities, on the other was senseless dreaming. How could I keep a perfect balance? Not let reality affect my dream, and not let my dream distort reality?

I'd care for my daughter the best way I knew how and treat her as if she would live. Leukemia was incurable, I knew that, no one would let me forget. But I would fight off one attack at a time.

That evening I returned to the hospital as stubborn as ever. I wanted to communicate to Mona all the life seething inside me. I wanted to speak of the future with her. I was ready for a show-down with the medical men.

"If Mona can eat," the doctor promised, "I'll let her go home."

The next day, from the public telephone, Mona proudly announced, "I ate everything on my plate — just about everything, anyway!"

She described the food she had been able to eat. The pediatrician signed her release that very evening. Too impatient to wait a minute more, we all hurried down to the hospital to pick her up. Even the dog was in on the celebration.

How do you live when every day that the sun comes up is a gift? You tear open the present without worrying. We just wanted to see, hear, feel everything. Every day was wonderful and we lived it as though it would never end. But at the same time, we took precautions as though each day would be the last.

Bent over my sewing machine, in the middle of making myself a dress, I thought of how much I wanted to live life to the hilt. I wouldn't stand for hatred; I wanted to love — but how could you fight without hatred?

Last night, I had said to André. "You're not going to go to sleep just like that, are you?" Some silly thing or other that I had done had gotten his back up. Why lose a night? I would have gotten down on my hands and knees to keep that from happening.

"No, you don't understand! I'm not saying we have to make love. I'm telling you I want you to understand me."

But I was a mystery to him. I was always overdoing things, and he was getting tired of it. I had accused him of only taking the parts of me that agreed with him, when he wanted to.

"It's all or nothing with you. No half way." But in the end, we shared an experience full of magic and happiness.

The dress was taking shape before my eyes. I hummed a love song and smiled. Mona was in a corner playing with the remnants of the cloth and her half-naked Barbie doll.

"Poor Mo, you really do look terrible with those stray hairs hanging down. If you like, I'll trim them for you."

She nodded, and I stopped my work to trim the dead hairs. They would soon be replaced by new hair. Mona's skull wasn't white any more like an old man's; it had turned dark grey.

114

Thousands of hairs would come back in a few days. Just like they had disappeared.

I held her out in front of me like a picture, to get a better look at her. In the light of love, I saw her as she would look in a few weeks, with her cheeks less swollen and a light down covering her head again.

"Just wait and see, you'll be pretty again."

Mona believed me and her eyes sparkled.

It was one of those days when everything I did was a perfect success. Standing in front of the mirror, I checked out the dress. It fell perfectly. I wanted my life to be filled with days like this one, days when your mind knows exactly what it wants. Suddenly I couldn't hold back my joy any longer. "Mona! Mona!" I cried out with sheer pleasure.

Mona was no stranger to my happy exclamations. She turned around just in time to hear me tell her how much I loved her.

I had been on cloud nine ever since the doctor announced that the blood tests had finally shown normal results. He prescribed medication that would keep the white cells at a set level. Now I could reduce the cortisone, and we would finally see Mona's real personality again. The cortisone had made her so irritable. We were set to finish it on New Year's Day.

The doctor said, "I'm sure you'll have a lovely holiday."

"You bet we will! Every day will be a holiday."

"After Christmas, we'll decide on a treatment that will keep her in remission."

There was that word: remission. We had reached the first step; I could stop and catch my breath now. It was time for a little celebrating. My dress would be ready in time for the Christmas dance at André's school.

The dance floor was buzzing with people eager to have a good time, including me. Only someone who'd lived like a hermit for months on end could appreciate the sight of old friends this much — not to mention the gin! I went looking for people I hadn't seen for so long. They greeted me with affection — and questions. Too many questions.

"How's your daughter?"

"She's fine, thank you."

They looked at me in surprise, almost disappointed, so I hurried to add with a bit of sadness in my voice, "For now, anyway. Of course, they can never be sure with . . ."

Did I really have to go and say that? I was mad at myself. But there was something arrogant about that "fine, thank you." I wished I had prepared some kind of pat answer that would have spared me from thinking about it and getting sad just to satisfy my friends' natural curiosity. Why hadn't I realized it would be like this? All I had thought about was the good time I was going to have.

"She's fine. I have a very good baby-sitter looking after her. She'll call if anything's the matter," I said to the next person who wanted to be filled in.

I said the first thing that came into my head to the rest of them. "I feel like dancing. Don't you think they did a nice job decorating the room?" And in the end people forgot to ask me about Mona. They could tell she was doing very well, thank you.

I had the feeling that a few proper old ladies in the corner were keeping a close eye on me. They must have thought I'd lost control when the rhythm of the music began to take over. Maybe they thought I was pretending. Their skeptical looks didn't bother me. I let the music move me. My head marked the beat, my hips suddenly remembered how to dance and my feet took the right steps without having to be reminded. I felt like a young girl again. Head spinning, out of breath, I hummed along with the songs. My heart hadn't pounded so hard out of happiness for a long time. My partner spun me around, came close, then pushed me away, all to the wild rhythm of the rock and roll music.

I gulped down a few lungfuls of air as André's arms surrounded me for an Elvis Presley slow dance. With his face against my neck, he said to me, as tender as the music, "We'll never let each other go." And in a dark corner of the room, I felt as if the earth had stopped turning and was just about to start revolving the other way. André kissed me.

With an hors d'oeuvre in my mouth, a glass in one hand and a full plate in the other, I was about to replenish my energy, when suddenly the manager of the hall came up to me.

"Please come to the phone. Someone wants to speak to you."

"I'll get it," André said, putting down the plate that he had been loading down with cold cuts. He followed the woman and I realized that I wasn't afraid. I didn't have that sinking feeling that an emergency usually brought on. Was I just too numb? I couldn't wipe that indecent satisfied smile off my face. I started guessing what was behind the phone call. Leukemia victims bleed easily, so I should have been worried. The only person who would call me was the baby-sitter. Something must have happened at the house, but not necessarily a crisis. If Mona had woken up and demanded to see us, the baby-sitter wouldn't have hesitated to call us.

Strange that that was exactly what had happened, I said to myself when André came back and described the conversation. We went home, but not before I insisted on inviting some friends to finish off the evening at our place with coffee and liqueurs.

André was in the middle of helping me undo my dress when the doorbell rang. They had come after all, just like they used to. I was glad. There was even a new couple with our old friends.

Feeling happy and lighthearted, I served everyone and sat down to chat. Then Mona got up. She came to rock in her little chair in the living room. A big photo of her from when she was three hung just above her. It was like one of those before-and-after ads. I wished I had hidden that picture. Not thinking it could be the same little girl, our new friends asked who she was. "What's wrong with their daughter?" I heard them whisper.

There were already a few anxious faces, but I refused to acknowledge them and left the others with the responsibility of answering that question. As if she felt their discomfort, Mona ran into my arms.

If I kept her out of sight, our friends would feel better about enjoying themselves. For my own good as well as hers, I said, "Go to bed now. We're back and there's nothing to worry about."

Mona tried to catch her father's eye, but he was with some other grown-ups, laughing away. Mona knew I was serious. She hesitated a moment, then jumped down from the chair. "Good night, my big balloon!" I said, giving her a friendly tap on the bottom.

Mona pretended to be very insulted by the nickname. But much to our guests' surprise, we both burst out laughing. We'd learned to laugh about her temporary deformity; it wouldn't last long. Mona's waxy cheeks and fat belly would disappear. As if we shared a special secret, my daughter and I kissed each other goodnight. Then she ran up happily to bed.

"Come by on Christmas Eve. There'll be plenty to eat and drink."

I invited everyone I could, and they felt obliged to visit us, the same way you'd feel obliged to go to a funeral. They celebrated Christmas as if it were the Last Supper. But they missed the point; we wanted a real celebration.

Since I was the only one who treated her as if she was in good health, Mona had become difficult whenever we had company. The more people paid attention to her, the more impossible she became. It wasn't even midnight and the house was in total chaos. Some of my guests had gone into the bathroom to cry in peace.

Her grandfather sniffled, "What has happened to my little granddaughter, she doesn't look like herself at all. Won't she ever get better?"

It really was an ordeal to see that strange-looking girl dashing through the house. She would become petulant, stubborn, or throw a tantrum about nothing. Her cheeks were swollen and waxy, as if they would split open. I was tempted to ask her to smile with a little less exuberance. And then there were those few straggly hairs floating around her head. The wig, of course, was warming one corner of a chair.

Who wouldn't be frightened?

My guests had wanted so much to cheer me up, but you have to know how to feel happiness yourself before you can give it to others, and their laughter was forced and nervous. They drank to jack up their courage until it was time to leave. I tried to calm them down.

"Mona had a good blood test before Christmas."

120

"Is that so?"

They didn't want to talk about it. It was all too much for them, and I could see the fear in their eyes. They thought I was crazy, that I didn't realize what was happening.

Suddenly I just wanted them all to leave. As someone went to get their coats I held on tightly to André's arm, because I could feel myself slipping into despair. But in the end, nobody even noticed that I had weakened for that split second.

A few days later, I went to a family reunion by myself. André was looking after the kids so I could have a change of scenery.

A young cousin came running up to me. "Is it true Mona's gonna die?"

"Who told you that?"

"The grown-ups."

I raised my voice so that everybody in the room could hear. "What kind of a thing is that to say! You're lucky that Mona didn't hear you. She was very sick, but now she's getting better. Never repeat anything like that. Would you like someone to say you were going to die if you were sick?"

"No."

He looked at his father who had spilled the beans. He didn't know who to believe. I made up his mind for him.

"Promise me you'll never say that again."

I couldn't even repeat the words, they were so dismal. But I wasn't having anyone predicting Mona's death.

Was I right? Who knew? The constant struggle was wearing me down, and I decided to go home. The rest of them insisted that I stay, but at the same time, they were glad that I was going so they could sit around and discuss my maternal blindness.

As for me, I was just stubborn enough to teach Mona a New Year's song. "We've got a dog at our house, We have fun at our house . . ." Mona sang it for everyone. All the finest voices in the world couldn't have been more beautiful. A month ago only scratchy noises had come from her throat; now she was singing. Holding back tears of joy, everyone in our house applauded.

Someone sent us an article about leukemia which said that the three-year survival period was an average figure. And at the bottom of the page it said that fifty percent of those who reached three years could get as far as five.

I didn't know whether I wanted time to pass quickly to reach the end of those three years or to slow down the clock in case we weren't part of the lucky half. Anyway, I refused to spend my time counting; it got in the way of life.

When we went to the hospital for the monthly injection, I took the article to show to the doctor.

"Look at this. The new growth of hair can even be saved. They explain it all here."

But it was time for the cold shower of reality. "Listen," he answered. "This article was written by the Cancer Society. More money is needed for this kind of research. It might not be very scientific."

All the same, he promised to get some information about the hair problem.

Every month I helped the doctor wrap a turban around Mona's scalp. Then the turban was filled with air. It had to be kept like that under pressure during the injection and for the five long minutes that followed. The toxic part of the medication was carried right to her head by her bloodstream, and we protected her scalp by keeping the drug from spreading through it.

"Does it hurt, Mona?"

Under the enormous cloth, she shook her head. To help her be patient we counted the final seconds with her until it was all over.

Now we turned every monthly visit into a holiday. We kept the car and went for a drive in the morning. After the injection, we treated ourselves to a good lunch. And then came the moment that made me happiest of all, when the lab announced, "Blood composition: NORMAL."

The holiday lasted all month. Mona took cortisone just for the first five days; the rest of the time she only had one little pill to swallow every evening. Plus a prayer to Saint Joseph, of course.

To chase away dark thoughts of the future, I kept my mind on next spring. I made plans. I even considered going back to work to help make ends meet.

Joey, my brother-in-law from California, came to pay us a visit.

"Let's go into town. Today is Mona's shot day. Come with us."

This was her second monthly injection. The doctor examined Mona carefully and raised his eyebrows at my carefree manner.

"How has she been doing?" he asked me.

"Pretty well, except that she always seems to be out of breath. Almost like she's trying to catch her breath after a race."

Once the examination was over, he told me, "Don't bother waiting for the results. I'll call you later."

The three of us went to have lunch in town and do a little window-shopping. But once I returned home, worry got the better of me. Why hadn't the doctor been willing to tell me the results right away? Maybe because Joey had been with us.

He finally got around to calling me two days later.

"Hello, Doctor. I was starting to get impatient. But we've taken so much of your time these last few months that I didn't want to call you at home just to hear that the results were still positive." I went on talking and he couldn't find a way to cut in. Obviously, he had something to tell me.

"There's no point hiding anything from you."

"What's there to hide?" Suddenly, I understood. "What's wrong?" I gasped.

"Mona's spleen and liver are still swollen."

"How was her blood test?"

"Normal."

"What's the matter then?"

"The liver and the spleen are the first signs."

"The first signs of what?"

"Please, you understand, don't you?"

Suddenly I let loose. "You told me to stop worrying! You told me her remission would last. It can't be over yet, it just started! Two months, Doctor!"

"I know, I know. I'm very sorry, but there's nothing I can do. Come back tomorrow. We'll do a marrow tap and start over again."

Sitting by the cursed telephone, I was haunted by the memory of something terrible I had done the day before. I had slapped Mona. This was my punishment. That would teach me not to strike my daughter. I'd lose her for good. I pictured the scene again. Mona, writhing on her bed and my hand raised, ready to come down on the stubborn little girl. If only I could just wipe away the whole thing!

But I had had my fill of Mona's tantrums and I wanted to teach her how to behave the next time. What next time?

I had given her a pair of sunglasses as a present. She had really wanted them and put them on right away. I was waiting for my thank you. Spoiled child that she was, she had forgotten what thank you meant, and her ingratitude got on my nerves.

"Say thank you or I'll take them away."

She was determined not to say anything that she didn't feel like saying. The more I talked, the more she withdrew.

"I spend my last dollar on you and you don't even thank me! You're so selfish." I raised my voice, not knowing if anger or love was taking hold of me. "Is that any way to grow up? Well, I'm not going to let you turn into a selfish little monster who no one will love, and who can't love anyone else either. So say thank you."

What an indignity, Mona must have thought, me getting mad at her. She grew more stubborn. She pushed me to the limit, to be the way I would have been with any other child. There was a challenge in her eyes.

I grabbed the sunglasses from her and she began screaming in protest.

"Go throw your tantrum in your room. That's right, go to bed, and stay in your room until you're in a good mood."

Mona wasn't about to move a muscle, that was clear. But I

wasn't going to give in either, and I grabbed her and carried her to her bed. She was fighting and it was all I could do to control her.

"Stop it or I'll . . ."

Smack! My hand struck her. Francis came running.

"What are you doing?"

The sight of Mona drove him to tears, as if I had just cut her throat.

"You're hitting my sister," he said, beside himself. "You know she's sick and you're still hitting her!"

I turned my back to him quickly to hide my tears. Finally I gathered up my courage and said, "You'll stay right here, Mona. You'll come out when you're ready to say thank you. Then I'll give you back your sunglasses. Not a second before, understand?"

She didn't understand anything. Her cries were heart-breaking.

Later, encouraged by her brother, she finally said thank you. And as if an enormous burden had been lifted from her shoulders, she threw her arms around my neck.

"Thank you, Mommy, thank you very, very much," she said.

I was still sitting by the phone, staring at the living room rug, when Mona ran by. I caught her by the arm.

"Come here!"

I examined her hands: they were pink. The insides of her eyelids were stretched tight and red with blood. Mona never liked me to play doctor with that serious look on my face. She twisted and turned, she couldn't sit still.

"Go on and play, you little rascal!"

My heart was pounding, but I wouldn't give in to panic. How could I be so carefree; I should have been breaking in two. Why didn't I feel anything any more? Had I finally had my fill of pain? Why was I so peaceful inside?

I had learned to take life day by day, hour by hour. Now it was dinner time. As if I hadn't believed a single word that the doctor had said, I washed the lettuce, leaf by leaf, very deliberately, as if to live this moment fully, and none other.

That evening in the bathtub, Mona had a healthy pink colour.

I called my brother who worked as a nurse.

"Aren't there any other diseases that would make the liver and spleen swollen?"

"Not very likely in her case. You'll have to trust the specialists."

The third biopsy was a lot less impressive than the first two. You can get used to anything, I guess. All the same, I had a nasty shock when I saw the doctor about to give Mona a shot of Vincristine. I knew the bottle, I couldn't be fooled. If he was starting to stuff her full of medication again, that meant only one thing: he was sure she had suffered a relapse. I knew I had to stop him, to stall for time.

"What are you doing, Doctor?"

"I'm giving her an injection."

"I know. But she just had one. It wasn't even a week ago."

"But we have to start all over again. The Vincristine I already gave her reduced the size of her liver."

God only knows how I had the gall to ask, "Why don't you wait until the results of the biopsy are in?"

He had been so good to Mona that I was ashamed of doubting him.

"I'm trying to spare her needless suffering," he explained. "She's sleeping now. Besides, that would mean another trip to the hospital."

That didn't matter, I could come back. I begged him not to give her a shot until the results were in. He seemed irritated by my persistence, but he washed the medication down the drain.

"Whatever you say. You'll have to go out of your way, not me."

I asked him to let me know about the results as soon as possible. Which is precisely what he did.

"Her marrow is healthy."

"I knew it!" I burst out.

He was exasperated. "Something doesn't add up. This swelling in her liver and spleen is abnormal. We'll just have to wait and see."

Once again we had to wait and see. In the meantime there was nothing to do but live as happily as possible. And dance — the dance of life, with Mona as my willing partner.

"Aren't you hungry, Mona?"

Would this never end? I was beside myself trying to find out what was wrong with her. Her skin was the colour of clay, and she was feverish now, too. We started out for the hospital. I had to do something.

The doctor was expecting us, and he looked pretty down. Mona was listless and apathetic, and as he lifted her onto the little white table once more, I said casually, "The edges of her eyes are all yellow, like she has jaundice. And her skin . . ."

Before I could finish, he stuck his head through the doorway and shouted to his secretary. "It's jaundice! Mona's got jaundice!"

The news travelled from one office to the next. From one nurse to another.

The doctor was smiling. Whatever for? Mona had jaundice and he was glad! He sat down to calculate the time that had elapsed since her last blood transfusion. That was the cause. Mona had caught jaundice from a donor. Jaundice was carried in the blood, the doctor explained, and nobody could tell it was there. A small infection was a little like indigestion. He talked at top speed, telling me happily that Mona would be very sick. She'd vomit a lot. He had a big smile on his face and his eyes were sparkling.

"Is she in danger?"

At least if I asked him a straight question, I might find something out.

"Oh, no! Not at all! Here's some suppositories to help treat her."

Happy as a clam, he added, "You know, it's a lucky thing we didn't give her the Vincristine. Her jaundice would have been much more severe."

Luck — is that what he called it?

Everybody at the nursing station was in a festive mood.

"It's jaundice," they told me happily.

They had all been following Mona's case, and they knew about the slowness with which she had reacted to the medication and the relapse that had seemed to occur scarcely two months later. From a medical point of view, the treatments had been a failure. No reaction to medication meant no remission. And no remission meant no survival. In their minds, Mona was back among the living. She was alive.

They had just learned something of the miracle of hope.

We went home, my heart blessed with an other-worldly sense of peace, as if I'd just understood something of the nature of miracles. I thought of what had happened in my mind, for that was where our miracle had occurred.

Not only had I been able to rid myself of that terrible anguish that overcame me every time the slightest alert sounded, but I never lost hope now, despite the odds. I was counting on better days, and I could picture them so clearly that I lived as though life held nothing but happiness for me. Waiting for happiness was happiness itself — a happiness that came from within. And I felt the benefits immediately: my heart was calm and my body more relaxed. I glanced around to the back seat. Mona was lying down, her skin yellow, struggling against her nausea.

"Mona, your mommy is happy; I know it sounds crazy, it makes no sense, but I'm happy!"

I hit the brakes suddenly. Mona began to vomit. She was as sick as a dog. She was constantly jumping up to run to the bathroom. We stood back quickly to let her pass. She didn't always make it and there were accidents in bed, but she never complained. Soon she would be feeling better — that's what her mother kept telling her. She could tell by the way people took care of her that she had nothing more than a good dose of jaundice. Soon it would be gone.

But I couldn't hide my sense of injustice at the sight of her trying to vomit. For the love of God, why did *she* have to be the one to get the blood that carried jaundice? As I cleaned up after her, I realized the difference between a struggle you undertake, knowing you're going to win, and a struggle you know you have no chance of winning.

"It'll soon be over, Mo darling. Just a few more days."

And the time would come when the jaundice was nothing but a bad memory.

It had been a snowy winter, but finally spring returned, as it always does. One sunny afternoon, Mona announced that she was now big enough to have a bicycle of her own. André and I exchanged a quick glance. Were we going to let her get covered with bruises from falling off a bike? Learning how to ride meant spending half the time on the ground, and with Mona, the slightest bump left its mark. Should we spare ourselves the sight of those bruises and her the needless pain? But what did that mean, needless pain? In this life you learned to fall down and get up again; she would learn that you could pick yourself up after a fall. And I would stop associating Mona's bruises and bumps with leukemia.

In his own way, André came to the same conclusion. Both of us thought in terms of life, not weeks or months. Mona was getting impatient; she pulled on my skirt.

"All right, Mom? *Please?* Look, everybody else has one. I want a bike, too!"

Everything happened very quickly, as it did every time her father and I agreed. Mona could scarcely keep up with us — that's how quick and determined we were as we walked to the corner hardware store, where handsome bicycles painted every colour of the rainbow were on display.

When I couldn't stand watching Mona fall down and get up again for the hundredth time in the back yard, I went inside and let her make her own mistakes, like any other child. That summer, under sunny skies, she ran this way and that, went swimming, played games. And we forgot to count the passing months. The days you don't count are the best ones of all.

In the fall, like all the other children, Mona went off to kinder-garten. Her satchel was hung by the door, her clothes were ready and her little shoes freshly shined. She was impatient to put everything to use. After one last day of waiting — a day that was too long for her and too short for me — she finally set out for school along with everybody else.

I waited for the right moment to have a word with the teacher who was going to be spending several hours a day with Mona.

"Miss, I would like to ask a favour." I did my best to speak casually, as I asked the teacher to pay special attention to Mona, but without giving her the feeling that she was being coddled or pitied.

"Can you let me know if any of your students have contagious diseases during the year? Like measles or chicken-pox. You know, childhood diseases."

Next I tried to tell her about Mona's illness. I had to. I said the word "leukemia," then took it back by pointing out how well she was doing. I asked the teacher to let me know immediately if there was the slightest sickness in the classroom, but just as a precaution. The doctor had insisted that this be done so that he would be able to take the necessary steps.

Mona wasted no time proving that she was in good health by winning first-place in the fifty-yard dash. It was wonderful to see her holding her blue ribbon, with her rosy cheeks and her curly hair which was only a few inches long. She was out of breath but full of life. I grabbed my championship runner and spun her around. Our laughter rang out as one. We shared the same indescribable joy: the joy of life.

We always told the doctor about all our exploits so that he too could share our delight. Every month we had a new story to tell him, and the anti-leukemia shots were accompanied by our happy conversation. The doctor laughed along with us, of course, but from time to time he considered it appropriate to bring me back to reality.

"Try not to be too optimistic."

He would speak those words of warning just as I was about to launch into another month, buoyed by Mona's normal blood test. Had he discovered something wrong? Why was he telling me that? He must be hiding something from me, some catastrophe! But he wasn't keeping anything from me, I'd just have to learn to close my ears. If I didn't, the doubt would make my life intolerable. Sometimes it would creep up on me as I watched television in the evenings, and by the time I had shaken off the nightmare, the program would have come to an end. I would sit there, staring at the screen, assailed by doubt. Could I be mistaken? Had Mona been less energetic these last few weeks? No — I was the tired one and my fatigue had made me anxious. Hadn't she begun coughing again? But Mona had as much right as any other child to catch a cold. I couldn't let my fears get the better of me, even though the sound of her cough brought back all those memories of a few months earlier — the temptation to pour her a big dose of syrup, to coddle her like a patient on her deathbed. But I wasn't about to start that painful existence all over again.

To calm myself down I went in to watch her sleep. She was a healthy colour, the colour of life. There was no fever. She'd be on her feet again in no time.

"Did you hear about that famous actor whose little boy had the same sickness that Mona has?" a friend said to me one day. I couldn't resist; I just had to listen, thinking it would be a hopeful story. The woman told me how the rich actor had taken his son on a trip around the world. A long, enchanting voyage. Captivated by the story, I pictured father and son embarking on a marvellous journey like in a fairy tale.

I didn't even wait for the end of the story. "Did his son get better?" I asked.

"Oh, no! he d--"

"Forget it!" I cut her off.

It was my own fault for listening. As soon as I caught myself reeling toward doubt, I made myself think of something else.

Rich or not, I'd never take a final journey with my child. Once you knew it was your last, it could never be happy. A trip was fun when you met new people and opened up new horizons. I imagined travelling to exotic places like New Mexico. One of these days we might just go there, the whole family.

Mona found me lost in these bright thoughts. She had come back from school in a good mood. Between bites of an apple, her eyes sparkling, she told me about all the new things she had learned, each one more exciting than the next.

"Mom, I know how to count. Mom, I can read. Mom, I have friends, too."

And thinking of my own discoveries, I answered, "It's exciting to learn new things, isn't it, darling."

To learn how to master my body — and my mind — I started doing yoga. For my family's well-being, I had to feel comfortable in my body and in my mind. In my heart, I realized once and for all that I was the soul of my family.

But I wasn't about to become a prisoner in my own house. I wanted to branch out, to fill my days in a way that would bring me some tangible benefits: like a pay cheque, for example. But could I do that if it meant being at home less often and leaving the children in the hands of a baby-sitter? And what about Mona? I wouldn't be as attentive to her needs and she'd miss me. How selfish I was, my maternal instinct kept saying. Had I already forgotten the gnawing feeling of guilt, when it's too late, when we wish that we had only known better?

But I had sworn to treat Mona as if she were going to grow up. I didn't want to be one of those mothers who clung to the dreams they invented for their children because they had never learned how to realize their own.

As I stacked the freshly washed sheets in the linen closet, I decided to do a little shaping up of my own life. From now on I would stop asking myself when my time to be happy would come. Later, when the children were grown? When I was rich? When I had more room to breathe? No — today was what mattered. I wouldn't waste any more time. I wouldn't try to live through my husband and children as I knocked myself out with nicotine, coffee and valium. I wanted to break new ground for Mona, the woman of the future.

Ideas like that couldn't help but cause a few problems. We were trying to learn to share the household chores, even though I ended up with the biggest slice of that pie. I had trouble making the others see things my way.

"I'm too tired," Mona would complain.

Six years old and she already knew my weakness better than I did. This damned fear of mine that kept coming to the surface: the relapse foreseen by the doctors and backed up by their statistics. Since I couldn't make her do any chores, I couldn't ask her brother to do any either. In the end, I gave in.

"It's all right, don't bother. I'll get along. Go out and play."

Winter was back already. The months had passed too quickly for us to notice. They were punctuated by a visit to the hospital, which provided us with a day off. Mona was dressed in a red hat and red pants. Her American grandmother had sent her a white rabbit coat and it contrasted beautifully with her black hair. Mona ran to kiss her pediatrician.

"Today," he said, "I've got some good news for you."

He took Mona on his knees. "These shots you've been getting every month, well, today is the last one. No more from now on. How does that sound?"

Mona threw her arms around his neck.

"From now on, she'll take one pill a day," the doctor said. "I'll let you decide when she should have a blood test."

He gave me some information about low hemoglobin. "Look at the lines on her hand. Stretch her fingers. The lines should be reddish, the way they are now."

He gave me a friendly pat on the shoulder, telling me again not to hesitate to call him if I felt the least bit concerned. Then he watched us go off, his fingers crossed for luck.

"Thank you, thank you so much, doctor," I said happily.

I had to keep myself from cheering. What an incredible victory! Mona and I practically ran down that interminable hallway that had so often been witness to our bent heads and heavy hearts.

Later at supper, the whole family was cheered by the good news. We were all brimming over with life and felt like jumping for joy. André decided to organize a football game in the hallway that ran along the dining and living rooms. It provided a twenty-four-foot-long playing field. Mona was the receiver. The teams were formed and, like any good housewife, I sighed, "Come on now, you're going to scratch the floors."

One look from André told me that the children's memory of a football game with their parents was worth more than a few scratches on the parquet. And the game began. Mona caught the pass as I tried to intercept it by blocking André. We played many games like that, both soccer and football, until the day the front window broke into a thousand pieces.

The basement was turned into a hockey rink and Mona into a goalie. A strange-looking goalie with two braids sticking out from under her mask. She was wearing her brother's pads and could stick out one leg as quick as a flash.

"What a save, Mo!"

Not only was she good in sports, she was graceful, too. She signed up for a figure-skating course and won six badges in her first season.

Mom, why do I have to take a pill every night? I'm not sick."

"That's so you'll stay healthy."

"Oh! Good night."

"Don't forget to say your prayers, my big girl."

As I put away the little box of pills, I was sorry that we had to go through this every night. Two years had gone by since the shots had stopped, two years since she had started taking the pills. Always at the same time of day I brought her one with a glass of milk. Those pills were a constant reminder that the sickness lay in wait for us. Besides, they had given us a couple of good scares because they acted on the white blood cells, maintaining them at a low level that sometimes sunk too low. Whenever that happened the doctor would tell me not to worry, that the dose might just be too high.

Then there would be a few days with no pills, while we watched Mona even more closely to detect the slightest sign of a relapse, while I told myself over and over that she was in very good shape. But the magic slip of paper that confirmed it never came too soon. I had to hold myself back from literally snatching it from the secretary who of course had to give it to the doctor first. I followed close on her heels, hoping to catch sight of the figures.

The pediatrician would say, "Everything's normal. See, the white blood cells have gone up to four thousand. That's very good."

And I would breathe a heavy sigh of relief, and try once again to get used to these variations in Mona's blood make-up.

"I can't go on living like this, hanging by a thread."

And André would answer, "We're all hanging by a thread."

"But I feel as if my thread is stretched over Niagara Falls."

Mona was growing up very quickly. We were all moving ahead, with the occasional backsliding, and at times I felt like simply giving up — forget about participating in school activities, forget working, trying to make a good home life. Sometimes I just wanted to sit quietly in a corner like a high-priced piece of furniture. I'd be happy watching my husband make a way for himself, occasionally sticking out a leg to trip him, to keep him by me as long as possible. It would have been easy to hold onto him with guilt, but who wanted a trapped man?

As I went upstairs to put the kids to bed, I thought of all the things I would have to teach them: how to make their beds, how to wash themselves behind their ears, how to be tolerant. I could never do it alone; André would have to do his part too. Francis would have to learn self-confidence. And Mona would have to learn how to make haste carefully. She was going way too fast.

As I watched them put on their pajamas, I thought to myself that I would like to see them grow up without losing their child-like hearts. When all was said and done, they would have to learn to articulate their needs without being arrogant, to be polite without lying. Above all, they would have to learn how to forgive.

"Mona, you shouldn't go to bed mad. You know I love you even when I bawl you out. You should go to sleep in peace, not with a heart full of bitterness."

"I'm all right," she answered, looking away so I would leave her alone.

I felt that it was important that she sleep well if she were to stay in good health.

"Come on Mo, tell me what's bothering you."

Finally, holding back a smile, she said, "Don't you ever give up, Mom?" And with one arm around my neck, she recited her favourite prayer: "There are many differences between me and the people I love. Help me, Jesus, not to let those differences stand between us. Amen."

My philosophy course was starting in a few minutes and I hurried to leave the house.

"Good night my love, be a good babysitter," I said to André.

He shook his head, both happy and perplexed to have a wife who wasn't simply content to go shopping and see a film every once in a while. No, his wife had to take courses. What good would that do, I could just imagine him thinking as I closed the door. I had to find a way to stop sending the children back and forth like a ping-pong ball: now it's your turn, now it's my turn. . . . I had to find a way to show him the difference between a free woman who's happy to come home and a woman who's forced to stay home.

I must have managed to convince him of something last night because this morning Mona announced to the doctor, "You should see them, Doctor, my father and my mother are always kissing and hugging."

"Mona, no comments. Stick out your tongue and say ah, that's why you're here," I said, blushing.

Since the doctor carefully examined Mona at the slightest infection, a special relationship had developed between them. When you saw your pediatrician twice a year, you didn't really feel like talking to him. You suffered through the examination, eager to get it over with. But Mona was very much at ease with her doctor and she told him everything that crossed her mind. All he had to do was to ask her a banal question as he examined her ears and he was rewarded with a veritable flow of words. Right away, Mona forgot all about the examination. I could see the doctor laughing to himself as he felt Mona's spleen.

I had scarcely gotten over my daughter's indiscretion when the doctor said, "I'm tempted to stop it. I've been looking into the question for a long time, you know, and survival doesn't necessarily depend on the length of treatment."

"I . . . I don't follow you, Doctor. What are you talking about?"

"The medication. It keeps the white blood cells at a very low level and I think Mona could fight germs a lot better by herself. What do you say we stop the treatment?"

I had no complaints about that! But, timidly, I had to ask him the question that still haunted me. "Is there any possibility, Doctor, that your diagnosis was wrong?"

As he absent-mindedly leafed through Mona's enormous file, he declared, "No. Her marrow was shot."

Then he turned cheerful again, noting that we had just reached the three-year stage. We were now one of the lucky ones who would surely be granted a five-year remission. For Mona's pediatrician, the moment of victory had come: he crossed out the word "leukemia" in the diagnosis section of the blood test form.

"It's not necessary any more," he said.

And I had been waiting for this moment for so long, that I had already tasted the joy I felt now.

That evening I flushed the little white pills down the toilet along with my bad memories. And when I went to kiss the children good night, I whispered all those loving words to them that I hadn't had the chance to say during the day.

"I'm glad I have you, my son, and I love you . . ."

And I lingered a little longer by Mona's bedside, marvelling at how far we had come in the last three years.

Mona just turned eight. A little while ago, she took up the piano again, and she played with a special gentleness and sensitivity. One day, when she had finished playing a piece, she stood up and turned to us. We were all going about our business as usual.

Offended, she looked at us and declared, "How about a little applause? Thank you, thank you!"

And she bowed so deeply that her forehead practically scraped the ground.

"That was very nice, Mo, but we're not going to applaud every time you practise," I answered, though I was tempted to say that my heart cheered for every day she lived.

"Oh, I was just kidding," she answered, a little surprised by her own boldness. Then she ran off to get back at her brother who never stopped teasing her. Seeing them pushing and shoving, I ordered them gently but firmly to behave.

"Not so rough. Remember she's your little sister."

"Little, she's stronger than I am," Francis replied, gasping for breath as he put a hold on Mona that she skilfully escaped.

Yes, Mona was strong in every way. Even the boys respected her at school. She was also at the top of her class, which increased her self-confidence. She even played teacher and helped her friends.

The other day she told me what she wanted to do when she grew up. She wanted to be a nurse, or why not a doctor or veterinarian? And she dreamed of giving concerts, too. I watched her making faces in the mirror, changing her expressions as she changed vocations.

"Why don't you start by cleaning your room?" I suggested.

"Mom, how come all the great compositioners are men?"

"Not compositioners, composers," I answered, side-stepping her question.

Then before I could escape from her room which she had turned into a knick-knack shop, I had to give in to the little sales-girl's insistence and buy a few trinkets with Monopoly money. At the same time I thought about Schubert: he certainly hadn't composed while doing housework.

"Thank you very much, Madam, and do come back. Oh, wait! You forgot your change."

The specialists at the hospital were highly interested in our case, and I was asked to speak to a group of doctors and psychologists.

"But I can't tell you anything that you don't already know," I protested.

But the organizer insisted, pointing out that my experience could help others. How could I refuse?

Standing before the specialists, I answered very circumspectly, afraid I would seem insane if I disclosed all my secrets. All the same, I did talk to them about my principle of living day by day.

"Like an alcoholic?" they asked me.

"Yes, it's a little like that. But you also have to really want to succeed and put your trust in the future."

But it was the facts they were after. How I had reacted to this or that, what I had read on the subject. I was more than a little relieved when the meeting finally ended and everyone got up for coffee. Since I found myself next to a psychologist, I took the liberty of saying, "Maybe I went about it the wrong way, but it was the only way I could find to keep on going . . ." I guess I wanted someone to tell me that I had done the right thing after all.

And the psychologist answered, "I'm willing to bet that if you had left the hospital that first day convinced that your daughter wasn't going to last a year, that's probably what would have happened."

His words made me so happy that I scarcely heard the rest of what he said. Somebody *had* understood what I was trying to say.

Though she wasn't much interested in dolls, Mona was very maternal with Kiki's puppies. She witnessed their birth and gave each one a name according to its personality. She gave individual attention to them all, taking into account the temperament of the one that liked to sleep nestled against her neck or the little black one who was the friskiest of the litter. When Kiki had no more milk to feed her puppies, Mona was very good about letting them go. First, she offered them to the nearest neighbours so that she would have a chance to watch the puppies grow up.

Like her older brother, Mona got a job delivering papers once a week to earn herself a little pocket money. When Christmas time came, she was the first one to run to the store and carefully choose gifts for everyone. Lovingly, she wrapped them up in paper that she had decorated herself. Often the paper became more precious than the gift because she had worked so hard to make the wrapping as joyful as the feeling in her heart. We couldn't put the Christmas tree up too soon for Mona. She decorated her room and wanted to bring the holiday atmosphere to every part of the house.

"Mona please, no tinsel in the bathroom. Enough's enough!"

She insisted that the traditional Christmas Eve dinner take place at our house, and loved it when all the guests began to dance and sing around the piano. Her feet barely touching the floor, she danced a polka with Uncle Bertrand and a jig with Grandfather.

Later Mona celebrated Valentines Day by drawing a huge heart pierced by an arrow with the words "Mona loves ?? " on it.

"Now who might that be for?" I asked her as discreetly as possible. "Go ahead, you can tell me."

Mona blushed. That was way too secret to tell. Even the boy who was the object of so much love didn't know it was for him. But by the end of grade five, the blank space in the Valentine was boldly filled with his initials.

"Oh boy! Now we're getting serious," her father teased her.

And as for me, I had reached a point in my life as a woman where I had stopped fighting for my independence, since I already had it — almost, anyway. But I had a secret desire that I could scarcely admit, it seemed so insane. My children were growing up and we had just started to have a little financial breathing room and the chance to take a couple of trips. How could I go and have another baby and start washing diapers all over again? Besides, as people kept reminding me, shouldn't I at least have the decency to be afraid of transmitting the disease?

At the hospital, I was assured that Mona's disease wasn't hereditary, even if nobody was completely sure what did cause it. My positive feelings about myself and my body and seeing all those newborn babies made me dangerously vulnerable. Whatever the reason, I forgot my usual precautions and there I was, pregnant. I knew it! I'd never forget that night of marvellous wakefulness.

I slowed down my usual break-neck pace, wanting to taste every moment of my pregnancy, even the heaviness of the final months. I felt so happy believing in life, to the point of trembling as I felt the baby move inside my womb. My pregnancy gave me wings and I prepared the family nest for the new arrival.

Mona wanted it to be a girl and insisted on starting to paint her room. She helped me and it brought us closer together.

"Will I have breasts, too? When am I going to be able to have babies?"

And without waiting for my answer she added, "First I'll have to find them a good daddy like mine."

Finally the big day arrived, when our second son made his remarkable entry into this world, greeted by his father who shared in the joy by participating in the delivery. The children made a big sign that they hung over the front door: WELCOME HOME, MOM AND MARK.

But a newborn baby puts a lot of demands on a home. Each member of the family has to make a sacrifice for this little being whose fragility gives him certain rights. Much to her regret, Mona had to give up her privileged position and share her mother and father. We always seemed to have the baby in our arms. She was getting tired of hearing, "Wait, Mona. Hurry up, Mona. Mona, leave the baby alone."

One day, when she was feeling particularly left out, Mona wrote us a letter that she hung on the door of her room: "Dear Parents: Don't look for me tomorrow, you won't find me. I'm running away. I'm fed up! You never have a minute to listen to me. Mom doesn't even come and talk with me any more before I go to sleep. Your only daughter, Mona."

"I thought we had prepared her well enough," André and I said to each other, trying to avoid feeling guilty.

We went into her room, aware that each member of the family needed affection and attention. I felt like a fountain that never had enough water to quench everybody's thirst. As we bent over our sleeping beauty to kiss her, we noticed a little note she had stuck on her bedside table so it would be the first thing she saw when she woke up. She was an early riser and didn't want her usual good mood to get in the way of her decision. "Don't forget," she had written. "Tomorrow you're supposed to be mad and run away from home."

Mona's eyelids were fluttering lightly and she pretended not to hear our laughter.

The next day she was still determined to carry out her plan, despite our supplications. Francis, who was twelve now, said that he knew very well what Mona was going through. He'd been there himself.

"Let me see what I can do," he said.

He went in to see his sister in her room.

"Don't pack your bags yet, Mo. Come with me."

They decided to take a long walk, better to rail against their parents and bemoan their hard luck. They hung around the hockey rink long enough to make certain they would be late for lunch. We would be sure to be worried.

When they came back, I said, "Nice to see you again. I made your favourite lunch."

Mona looked confused. Finally, after we had finished eating, she announced that this time she wouldn't leave. She was about to set down her terms for staying, but didn't get that far. The whole family crowded around her and said, "You know we love you — even if we are always asking you to run errands for us!"

At her little brother's baptism, with deep feeling, Mona read part of *Jonathan Livingston Seagull* that she had adapted to the occasion.

"Higher, Mark, fly higher still . . ."

And her brother added his contribution: "There is more to life than eating or fighting or power . . ."

The newness of this little being filled me with such joy that I felt moved to fight to make the world a better place. The baby's fragile breath against my neck gave me a sense of continuity — a sense of man creating himself, a dream of reaching out for a world where good triumphed over evil, where love conquered hate.

Mona, the little girl with the seven-year-long remission, was about to give a recital with her friends from school. The room was filled with proud parents.

"Shhh! Mona's going to start."

My baby in my arms, I proudly watched my grown-up twelve-year-old girl play a piece that everyone in the family already knew

154

by heart, since we had heard her practise it so often. A special light was shining in my eyes, not because it was *my* daughter playing the piano so well, but because this scene, which I had so often dreamed of, had finally become a reality.

Tonight, our hair tangled together on the pillow, we dried our tears. This afternoon we found out that we had to start all over again. The hematologist confirmed it: Relapse.

We were not afraid. Together, we exchanged a vow: this chapter of our story would be the finest one yet.